U-2 SPYPLANE in action

By Larry Davis
Color By Don Greer
Illustrated By Perry Manley

Aircraft Number 86

squadron/signal publications, inc.

Francis Gary Powers flying CIA Article 360, a U-2B (56-6693), photographs Soviet Intercontinental Ballistic Missile sites at Sverdlovsk, Russia on 1 May 1960. Soviet air defense forces fired fourteen SA-2 Guideline surface-to-air missiles at Powers, destroying the U-2.

ISBN 0-89747-202-0

If you have any photographs of the aircraft, armor, soldiers or ships of any nation, particularly wartime snapshots, why not share them with us and help make Squadron/Signal's books all the more interesting and complete in the future. Any photograph sent to us will be copied and the original returned. The donor will be fully credited for any photos used. Please send them to:

Squadron/Signal Publications, Inc.
1115 Crowley Drive.
Carrollton, TX 75011-5010.

Acknowledgements

Air Force Museum
Lockheed California Company (LAC)
Mick Roth
John Andrews
David Menard, USAF Retired
Eric Schulzinger

Dedication

To the memory of U-2 pilots that gave their all for their country; especially Francis Gary Powers and Major Rudolph Andersen, USAF.
Special thanks go to Susan for pushing so hard.

A Lockheed U-2C of the Central Intelligence Agency in flight over the California mountains. Over the years the U-2 has come to be known to many as "The Black Lady of Espionage." (LAC)

N809X

INTRODUCTION

The Lockheed U-2 was conceived by Kelly Johnson, chief engineer of the Lockheed Aircraft Corporation and founder of the famous Lockheed "Skunk Works." Clarence "Kelly" Johnson joined Lockheed during 1933 upon graduation from the University of Michigan where he had been involved with wind tunnel tests of the Lockheed Model 10. During these tests he had formed an opinion that the Model 10 would be unstable. Being a new employee fresh out of college, Johnson was told by Hall Hibbard *"See if you can do any better!"* Johnson did and his design evolved into the famous Lockheed Electra. The brash young man became the sixth member of Lockheed's engineering team, and become Lockheed's Chief Engineer in 1938.

During 1936 the Army Air Corps issued a specification for a twin engined fighter aircraft with a top speed of 367 mph. Lockheed and Kelly Johnson met the specification with a design that evolved into the Lockheed P-38 Lightning, a fast, maneuverable fighter with a longer range than any contemporary US fighter. It was the speed and range of the Lightning that led Johnson into the field of aerial reconnaissance, and ultimately to the U-2.

Early in the Second World War the US Army Air Corps realized it needed an aircraft with both high speed and long range to carry out long range strategic reconnaissance against targets deep in enemy territory. Photographic information was needed on enemy industrial, military, and political complexes outside the range of single engine tactical photo aircraft. To meet this requirement Johnson mounted four K-17 cameras in the nose of a P-38; tests with the modified fighter proved successful and the Army ordered the modified P-38 into production under the designation F-4. The F-4 and later F-5 (late model P-38s) became the standard USAAF photo aircraft in Europe and the Pacific. High altitude, very long range missions and electronic intelligence missions, however, were still flown by converted bombers such as the F-7 (B-24) and F-13 (B-29).

Late in the war the first jet aircraft were introduced into combat by the Germans. The Messerschmitt 262, with its high speed (over 150 mph faster than Allied propeller-driven fighters) and heavy firepower was a giant technical advance. In the United States, the Bell Aircraft Corporation had built the first US jet aircraft. The XP-59, however, proved to be disappointing since its performance was only marginally better than existing propeller fighters.

Johnson had also designed a jet fighter utilizing a 3,000 lbst British engine. To preserve security Johnson had to move his engineering staff and quarters far from the Lockheed production lines. Using old engine crates to build a shop, Johnson and his staff worked around the clock, building the XP-80 Shooting Star in 143 days, thirty-three days ahead of schedule. The first of the famous Lockheed "Skunk Works"* aircraft was a reality.

The XP-80 prototype made its first flight on 8 January 1944 becoming the first US fighter to exceed 500 mph. With the introduction of jet fighters into the inventory, the Army Air Force issued a requirement for a jet powered reconnaissance aircraft. Lockheed responded by mounting an F-4 camera system into the gun bay of a YP-80A. The conversion was successful and the USAAF ordered the aircraft into production under the designation F-14A (later changed to RP-80A/RF-80A).

The need for a high altitude reconnaissance aircraft, one that would be immune to interception, became apparent during the Korean War. 5th Air Force RF-80s had the range for missions over North Korea. Reconnaissance of enemy bases on the Asian mainland, however, had to be flown by medium jet reconnaissance bombers and the RB-45 Tornado had proven vulnerable to interception by MiG-15 fighters.

Johnson went to Korea during 1952 to interview pilots who had fought MiG-15s. He returned to Lockheed determined to design the fastest, highest flying fighter in the world. Armed with the information he had gained in Korea, Johnson designed a radically new fighter, *the missile with a man in it* — the F-104 Starfighter. On 28 February 1954, Lockheed test pilot Tony LeVier flew the XF-104 to 103,395.5 feet, attaining a speed of 1404.19 mph. It was the fastest, highest flying fighter in the world. The XF-104, however, lacked the range and payload needed for reconnaissance missions.

Events in the Soviet Union during the early 1950s led the Defense Department to issue a requirement for a reconnaissance aircraft capable of overflying the Soviet Union at extreme altitudes. The requirement (Design Study Requirement No. 53WC-16507, dated 27 March 1953) called for a single seat sub-sonic aircraft, capable of carrying a 700 pound payload over 3000 miles at altitudes over 70,000 feet. The aircraft would be unarmed and no ejection seat would be fitted. The mission was daylight photo reconnaissance from extreme altitudes.

Three companies responded to the Air Force requirement. Martin Aircraft Company proposed a modified B-57 Canberra, while Bell Aircraft and the Fairchild Aircraft Company each submitted entirely new designs. The Martin proposal was accepted, although the RB-57 was to be an interim aircraft while work proceeded on a better design.

Lockheed had not been issued the initial requirement. The company, however, had conducted preliminary design studies (Lockheed Report 9732) on their own. On 18 May 1954, Johnson delivered this proposal to the Air Force. The Lockheed model CL-282 was based on XF-104 fuselage components mated with an extremely long wing. After evaluating Lockheed's proposal the Air Force rejected it based on the use of the experimental General Electric J-73 engine. The Air Force insisted that the aircraft use the proven Pratt & Whitney J57.

Rejected by the Air Force, Johnson decided to try and sell the design to other Defense Department agencies. In November of 1954, the design was submitted to officials of the Central Intelligence Agency. Following a meeting between CIA director, Allen Dulles;

Lockheed's first photo reconnaissance aircraft was the F-4/F-5 photo version of the P-38 Lightning fighter. This F-5, *STAR EYES* of the 28th Photo Reconnaissance Squadron, carries seventy-eight mission markings on the nose in Black. (AFM)

Lockheed built the first American tactical jet reconnaissance aircraft, the RP-80 (later RF-80) Shooting Star. RF-80As later flew combat reconnaissance missions over Korea. (Roberts via Foote)

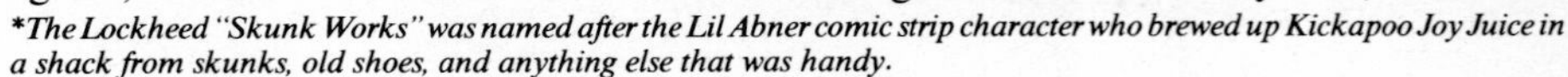
**The Lockheed "Skunk Works" was named after the Lil Abner comic strip character who brewed up Kickapoo Joy Juice in a shack from skunks, old shoes, and anything else that was handy.*

CIA Chief of Research and Development, Dr Joe Charyk; and Johnson, an agreement was reached where Johnson would re-design the CL-282 to use the Pratt & Whitney J-57.

Johnson redesigned the fuselage to accommodate the larger diameter J-57 still using F-104 technology. The two programs complimented each other since each stressed weight savings to gain performance. A manually operated side hinged canopy, similar to the F-104, eliminated the canopy hydraulic system. The F-104 ejection seat was eliminated since a pilot could not survive a bailout at proposed operating altitudes, and the fuselage cross-sections, air intakes, and tail were all based on the F-104.

Johnson had indicated that he could build twenty aircraft plus spare parts for $22 million, and that he would deliver the prototype within eight months of signing the contract. On 9 December 1954 the CIA awarded Lockheed a development contract under the code name Project AQUATONE. The highly classified project was funded from two different sources; CIA funds for the airframe, and Air Force funds for the engines (which were purchased under a B-52 spare engine contract). To preserve security the first contract payment ($1.2 million) went to Johnson's home *via the U.S. mail* and the prototype was not given a Lockheed model number, being known simply as CIA Article 341. A cover story was prepared explaining that the aircraft was a high altitude research platform for the National Advisory Committee for Aeronautics (NACA).

While the "Skunk Works" began building the hand made prototype, Johnson began searching for a location to test the top-secret prototype, which had been nicknamed the "Angel" by the Lockheed staff. A suitable location was found at Groom Dry Lake which was part of the Atomic Energy Commission's atomic test facility in the northwest area of Nellis AFB. By July of 1955 the test site, nicknamed "The Ranch" was ready, and so was the prototype. On 24 July 1955 the completed prototype was disassembled and prepared for shipment. The fuselage was covered with a tarp and loaded into a C-124 Globemaster; with the wings and engine being loaded into a second C-124. The prototype was then flown to Groom where it was reassembled and hidden in a hangar.

The prototype resembled a jet powered sailplane with a slender fuselage, long tapered wings, and tall fin and rudder. It was 49 feet 8 inches long with a wingspan of 80 feet 2 inches and height of 15 feet 2 inches. The prototype weighed 12,000 pounds empty, with a takeoff weight of 22,000 pounds. Article 341 was powered by a 10,500 lbst Pratt & Whitney J57-PW-37 turbojet burning a low-volatility, low vapor-pressure kerosene commonly called JP-7. The camera compartment ('Q-Bay') was in the fuselage immediately behind the cockpit. Access to the 'Q-bay' was made through two doors installed on both the fuselage spine and belly.

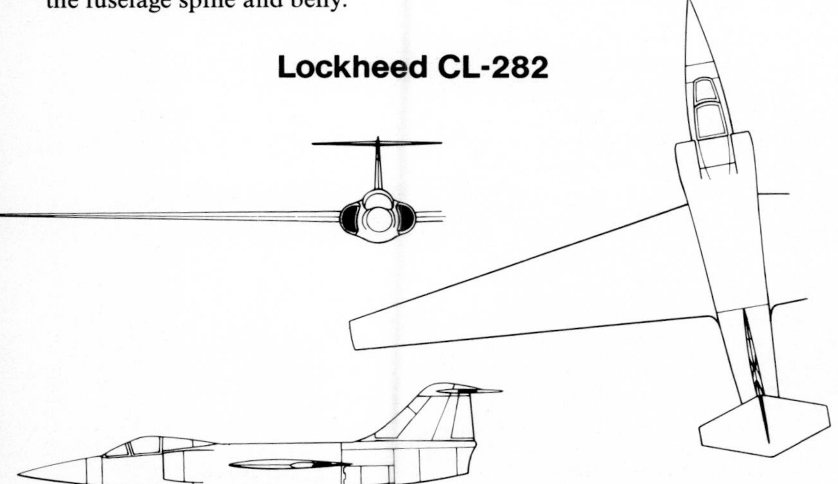

The U-2 prototype, known as Central Intelligence Agency Article 341, was officially accepted by the CIA on 8 August 1955. Although the aircraft carried military style national insignia, it was owned by the CIA. The prototype featured a sliding canvas cover inside the cockpit canopy to shield the pilot from the sun at high altitudes. (LAC)

The unorthodox landing gear consisted of tandem sets of dual wheels, similar to those found on the Boeing B-47, with the rear set being much smaller than the front main gear. To balance the wings, a set of dropable stanchions with small dolly wheels (called "pogos") were attached at mid-span on each wing. These fell away when the aircraft took off and were retrieved by ground crews to be reused when the aircraft landed. To protect the wingtips the prototype had small skids on each wingtip. To shield the pilot from the sun at high altitudes, a canvas sunshield was mounted on two support cords attached to the inside top of the canopy.

On 29 July 1955, Lockheed test pilot Tony LeVier began a series of taxi tests. During the third test, LeVier suddenly found himself some thirty-five feet above the runway. He had accidentally lifted off and now the aircraft didn't want to land. LeVier had to stall out the wing and the prototype hit the runway hard, blowing both main wheel tires and slightly damaging the tail wheel.

Repairs were quickly made and on the morning of 1 August 1955, the "official" first flight of Article 341, Lockheed serial 001, took place in front of every member of the Skunk Works that had worked on the project and a number of Air Force officers and CIA officials from Washington. LeVier made an uneventful takeoff, climbed to 12,500 feet and spent forty-five minutes testing the aircraft. Everything went smoothly until the landing. On the first two landing attempts the prototype porpoised. Finally LaVier made a full stall landing and the Article 341 settled gently onto the runway and rolled to a halt.

Early in the flight test program the prototype was assigned the Air Force designation U-2 (Utility 2). These early tests revealed that the U-2 was a demanding aircraft to fly. At mission altitudes there were only a few knots separating the top speed buffet and the stall speed buffet. This speed range became known as the "coffin corner" and required extreme care not to over-control. Recovery from a stall at mission altitude was difficult, if not impossible. The pilot could not bail out, since at altitude there is insufficient pressure to keep blood gases in solution. Oxygen in the blood evaporates, giving the appearance of boiling, and death quickly follows.

Landing the U-2 demanded skill and constant attention. Fuel in the wing tanks had to be balanced prior to landing to prevent a wing from dipping and ground looping the aircraft. U-2 landings are full stall landings and as the aircraft nears the ground the pilot cannot see how far off the runway he is. The pilot is assisted by a "Mobile Control" vehicle with a second U-2 pilot who follows it down the runway relaying the altitude to the pilot. After landing, the ground crew reattaches the pogos so the aircraft can be taxied.

The early tests established the U-2's flight envelope and had demonstrated that the U-2 was a stable camera platform at altitude. In 1955 there was nothing in the world that could fly with it at its normal operating altitudes -- not in the West or in the East.

Development

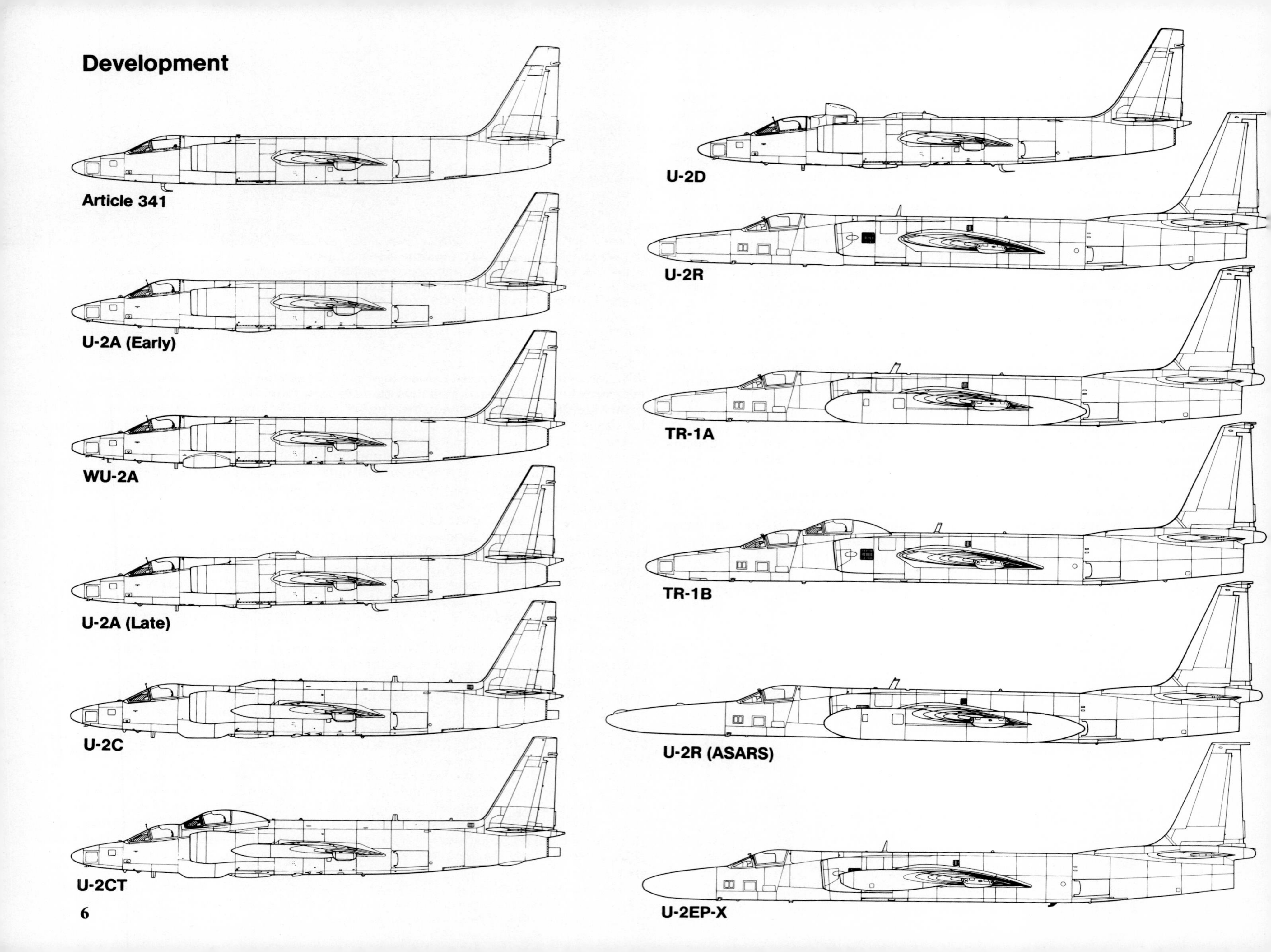

U-2A

After the U-2 prototype had successfully completed its initial flight test program during late 1955, the CIA ordered the aircraft into production. The initial contract called for twenty aircraft under the Air Force designation U-2A. Production U-2As differed from the prototype in a number of ways. The 10,500 lbst Pratt & Whitney J57-P-37 engine was replaced with a 11,200 lbst J57-P-31A engine specifically built for high altitude operation. The canvas sunshade in the canopy was replaced by a section of the upper canopy plexiglas which was painted White to reflect the sun. A broad, flat shaped fairing was added to the rear fuselage under the rudder which was used to house either a braking parachute or additional sensors. Early production aircraft were not fitted with ejection seats, although they were later retrofitted to all U-2 aircraft. U-2As were delivered to the CIA at Groom Lake in an overall natural metal finish devoid of markings except for necessary servicing stenciling.

All subsequent variants of these early U-2s were based on the production U-2A airframe. Since the number of aircraft to be built was never expected to be high, Lockheed never established a production line in the normal sense, with all aircraft produced being basically hand made airframes. With the many interchangeable modifications done to the U-2, it has become nearly impossible to state with certainty the exact model a specific aircraft within the U-2 series is, or was. Changes and reconfigurations of basic U-2A airframes were common, with U-2As being rebuilt as U-2Cs or U-2Fs and then later retrofitted back to U-2B configuration. Serial numbers were often reassigned and switched for security reasons. CIA, NACA, and NASA civil registrations were assigned at random and the same "N" number was often assigned to two different aircraft. Because of the security surrounding the program, total production figures are also difficult to state accurately. It is believed that at least sixty early U-2s were built, with fifty-three Air Force serial numbers having been confirmed as belonging to early U-2s.

As part of the security surrounding early production U-2As, this U-2A was fictitiously marked with National Advisory Committee for Aeronautics (NACA) insignia on the tail. NACA never operated U-2s, although its successor, the National Aeronautics and Space Administration (NASA) obtained several for high altitude research work. (LAC)

This overall Flat Black CIA U-2A carries false NASA tail marking and a false Air Force serial number on the tail in White. CIA aircraft normally were devoid of markings except during public display, when they often carried false markings. (GS Williams via Andrews)

Tail Cone Development

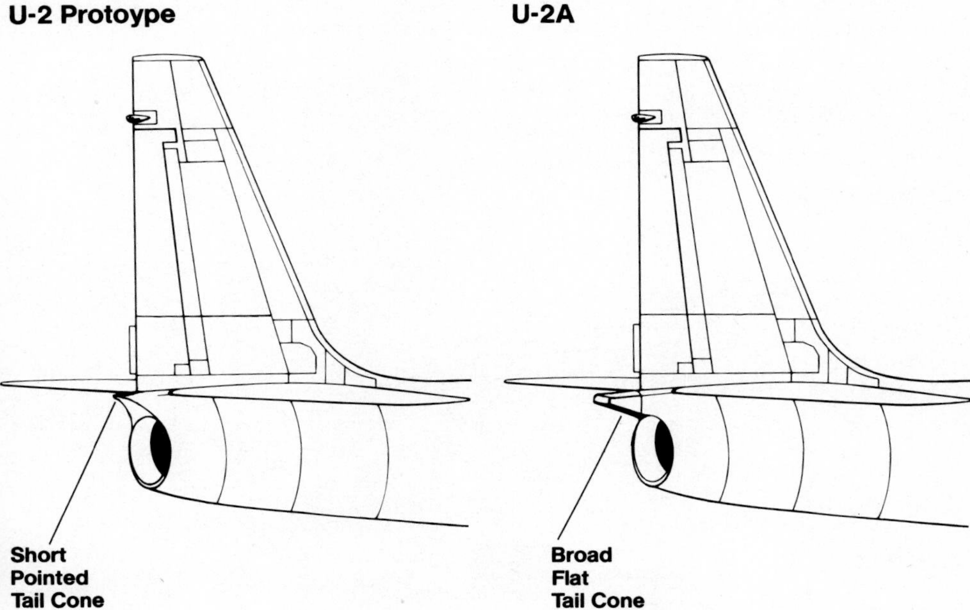

(Above) This U-2A (56-6696) was the first U-2 delivered to the Air Force, almost two years after the first U-2 was delivered to the CIA. The U-2s were delivered to the 4080th Strategic Reconnaissance Wing on 11 June 1957, in natural metal finish and full Air Force markings in Black. (John Andrews)

(Below) This U-2A of the Air Force Flight Test Center at Edwards Air Force Base is shielded from the sun by a "Howdah", a portable cover which was held in place on the fuselage by a curved frame with canvas retaining straps. (USAF via Andrews)

Canopy Development

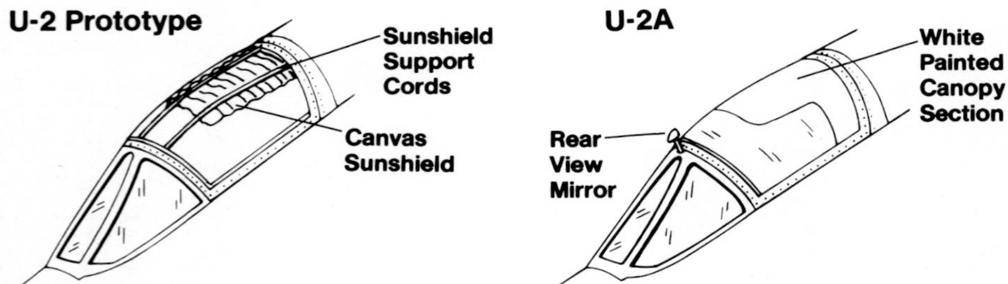

Early U-2 Variants

WU-2A

Five production U-2A airframes were modified for high altitude air sampling with an air intake mounted in the nose and a forward facing air scoop installed on the left side of the "Q bay", extending down below the the fuselage in a streamlined fairing. The air scoop housed filter elements that trapped fall out particles for later study. At least seven additional U-2As were later modified to WU-2A standards for use in the High Altitude Sampling Program (HASP). Other than the nose air intake and underfuselage air scoop, these aircraft were externally identical to the U-2A.

U-2B

At least seven U-2As were re-engined with the 15,800 lbst Pratt & Whitney J75-P-13A engine under the designation U-2B. Externally identical to the U-2A, these aircraft were internally strengthened to accept the higher thrust and increased weight of the new engine. Range, payload, and airframe fatigue life were all increased slightly. Ejection seats were added, these becoming standard on all U-2s.

U-2C

A number of U-2A and U-2B airframes were re-engined with the 17,000 lbst J75-P-13B engine under the designation U-2C. To accommodate the increased air flow demands of the new engine, the fuselage air intakes were enlarged, with slightly bulged contours. The nose was lengthened slightly to provide internal space for new sensors, internal fuel tankage was increased, provision was made for carriage of "slipper" style wing fuel tanks, and a dorsal equipment "canoe" fairing was added to the upper fuselage spine running from just behind the intakes to the base of the fin. An unspecified number of U-2A airframes still in production were completed as U-2Cs.

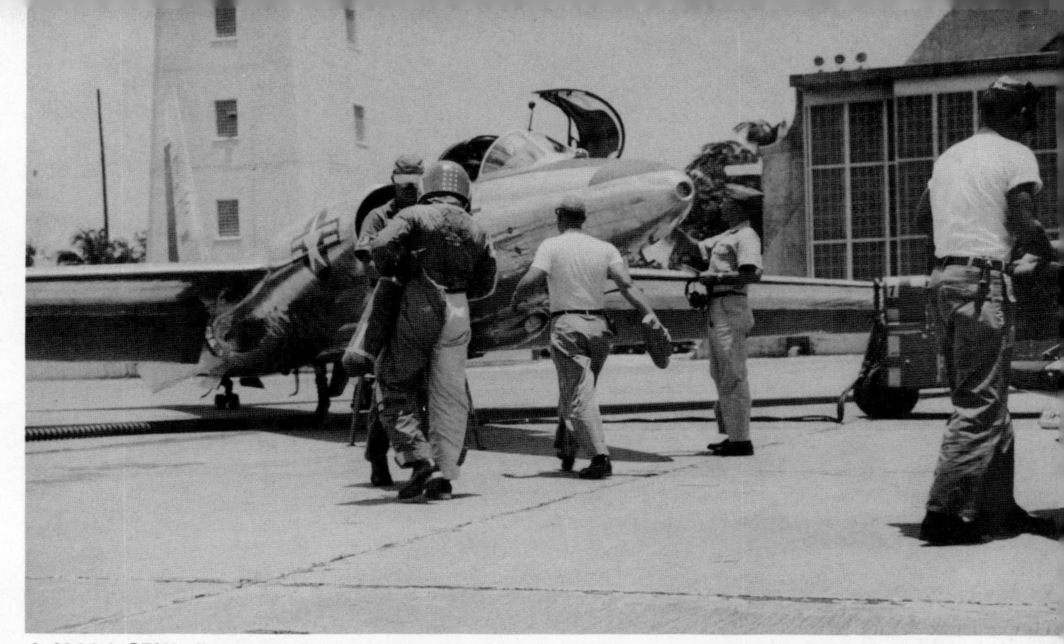

A 4080th SRW pilot prepares to board a WU-2A for a HASP mission out of RAAF Laverton, Australia. The small circular air intake in the tip of the nose is part of the HASP sampling system. The long rear view mirror on the canopy frame allowed the pilot to see if the U-2 was leaving a contrail. (USAF via Andrews)

The faired air scoop on the lower fuselage side is the intake for the High Altitude Sampling system installed in the "Q" bay as part of the HASP program. Filters inside the scoop trapped radioactive dust for later study. (Hopton via Andrews)

HASP Air Scoops

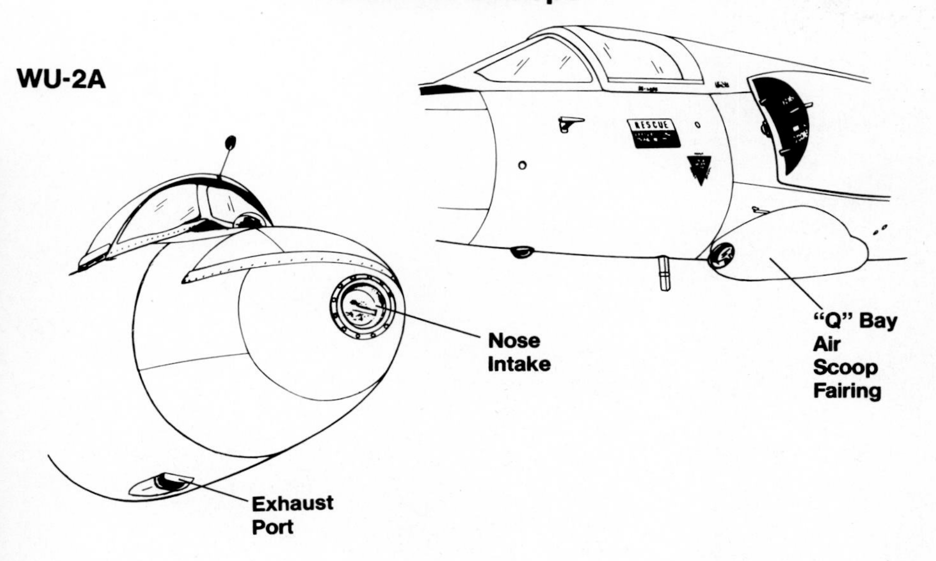

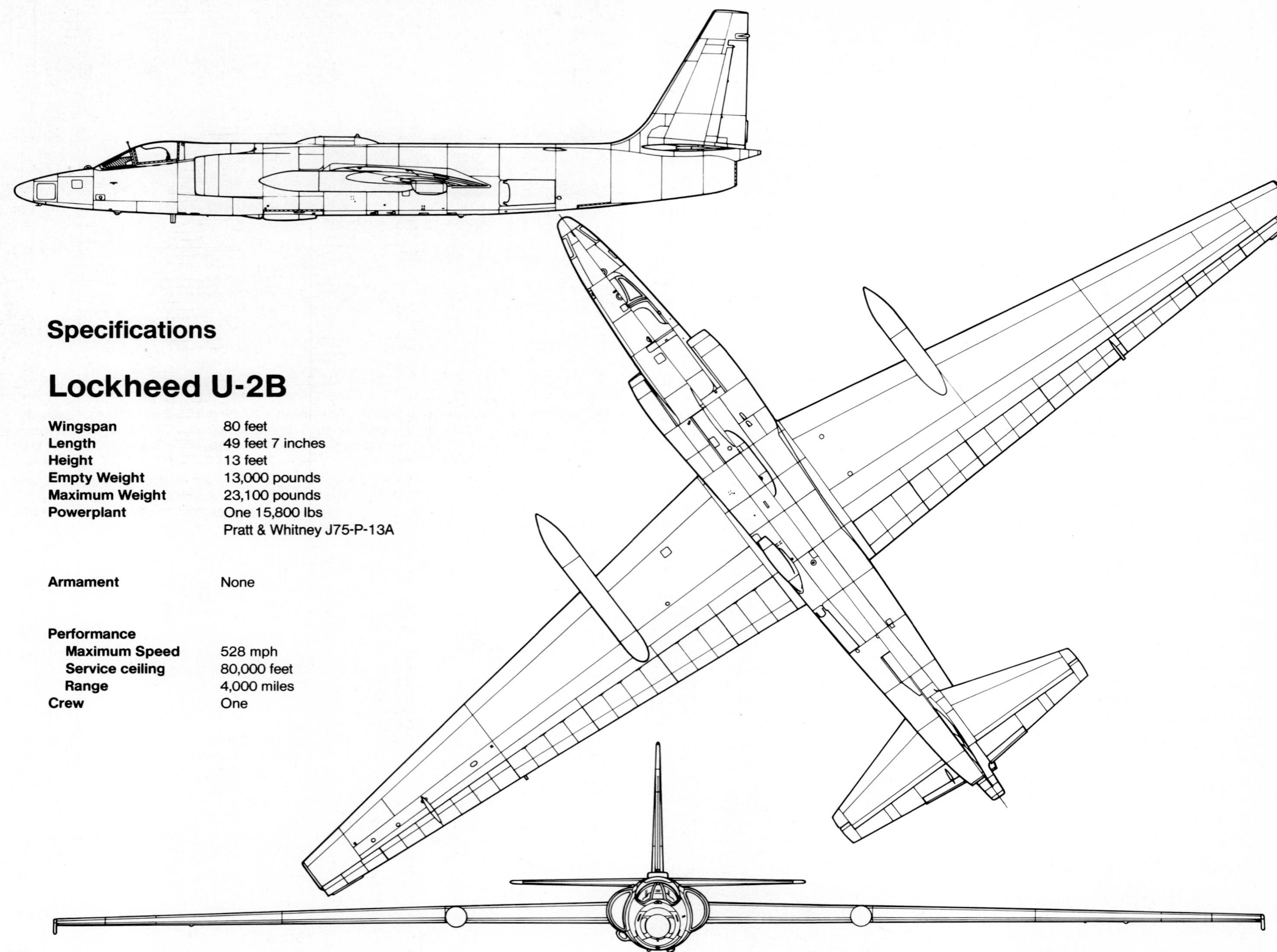

Specifications

Lockheed U-2B

Wingspan	80 feet
Length	49 feet 7 inches
Height	13 feet
Empty Weight	13,000 pounds
Maximum Weight	23,100 pounds
Powerplant	One 15,800 lbs Pratt & Whitney J75-P-13A
Armament	None
Performance	
Maximum Speed	528 mph
Service ceiling	80,000 feet
Range	4,000 miles
Crew	One

U-2CT

The U-2CT was a two-seat conversion of one U-2C airframe and one U-2D airframe. The U-2CT had a second cockpit installed above and behind the first cockpit with the crewman occupying the upper half the equipment "Q" bay. U-2CTs were used as flight trainers with all sensor equipment deleted.

U-2D

Five U-2A airframes still in production were completed with a modified systems "Q" Bay, which could house either a second crew member or alternate sensor systems. A rear hinged crew entry hatch with two small windows was installed on the upper fuselage spine behind the cockpit canopy in place of the upper "Q" bay hatch. Besides the five initial conversions, at least one other U-2A airframe was rebuilt to U-2D standards and one U-2D airframe was later modified to the two seat U-2CT trainer configuration.

U-2E

A number of U-2A and U-2B airframes were modified with J-75-P-13B engine, additional ECM equipment mounted in pods on the tail, and a small fuselage spine electronics "canoe" fairing. At least eighteen U-2A aircraft were modified to U-2E standards and were assigned solely to the CIA.

U-2F

Four U-2A airframes were modified for inflight refueling with a refueling receptacle mounted on the upper fuselage spine in the front of the dorsal canoe fairing. After a series of combat tests with the refueling equipment, these aircraft were retrofitted to U-2C stan dards with the refueling equipment deleted.

U-2G

Two U-2C airframes were modified for aircraft carrier operations with strap on arrestor hooks, reinforced landing gear and wingtip skids, and the addition of large spoilers to dump lift on landing. These aircraft were later retrofitted back to U-2C standards and assigned to NASA.

U-2J/U-2N

These designations are believed to have been designations reserved for modifications that were not standardized, or for aircraft that were modified with internal fixtures for installation of an arrestor hook for carrier operations. These designations remain unverified.

This Flat Black CIA U-2B has been modified with a sensor canoe on the fuselage spine and two blade antennas on the rear fuselage. The U-2B was a U-2A airframe re-engined with the 15,800 lbst Pratt & Whitney J75 engine. The only markings carried are the civil registration "N805X" on the tail in White. (LAC via Andrews)

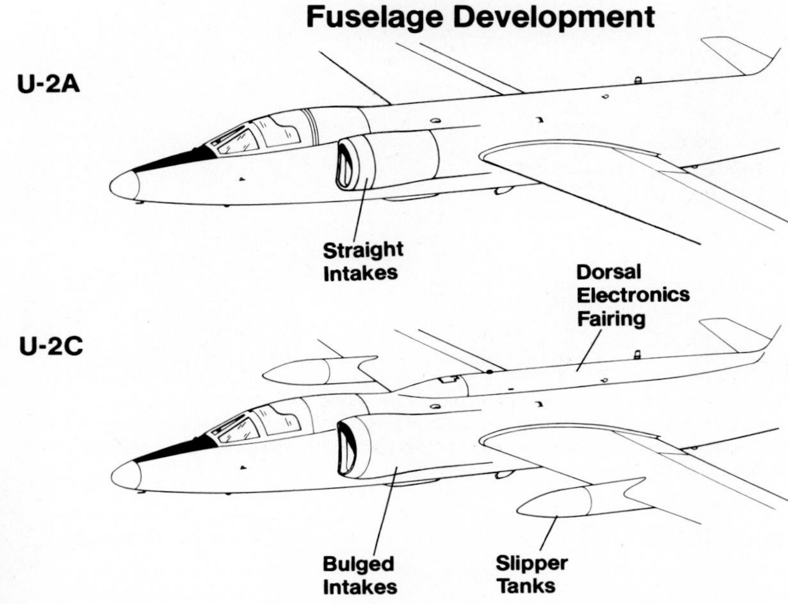

A ground crewmen removes the locking pins from the wing "pogo" wheels of this WU-2A of the 4080th SRW. The WU-2A was modified with an air sampling scoop under the equipment "Q" bay as part of the High Altitude Sampling Program, which collected samples of radioactive fallout in the upper atmosphere. (USAF via Andrews)

Ejection seats were retrofitted to all earlier U-2s after they were introduced on the U-2B. The early ejection seat was prone to failure at high altitudes because of hardening of the canopy from the frigid temperatures. Later seats were fitted with canopy penetrator spikes which solved the problem. (LAC)

The twin wheel wing "pogo" landing gear were secured to the wing with locking pins. When the aircraft was ready for takeoff the ground crew removed the pins which allowed the wheels to fall free. Upon landing the ground crew would re-attach the "pogos" so the aircraft could taxi. (Levy via Andrews)

The main landing gear of the U-2 retracted into wells on the underside of the fuselage equipped with bulged gear doors. The forward set of landing gears were equipped with brakes, while the rear set were not. (Levy via Andrews)

The rear main landing gear also served as a fully castoring tail wheel. U-2 pilots flew the U-2 as a jet powered "tail dragger" and landing approaches were made using techniques common to tail wheel configured aircraft. (Levy via Andrews)

A natural metal U-2C of the 100th SRW based at Davis-Monthan AFB. The U-2C featured a Pratt and Whitney 17,000 lbst J75 engine, bulged air intakes, dorsal electronics fairing, and updated sensor systems. (USAF via Andrews)

Infrared Deflector

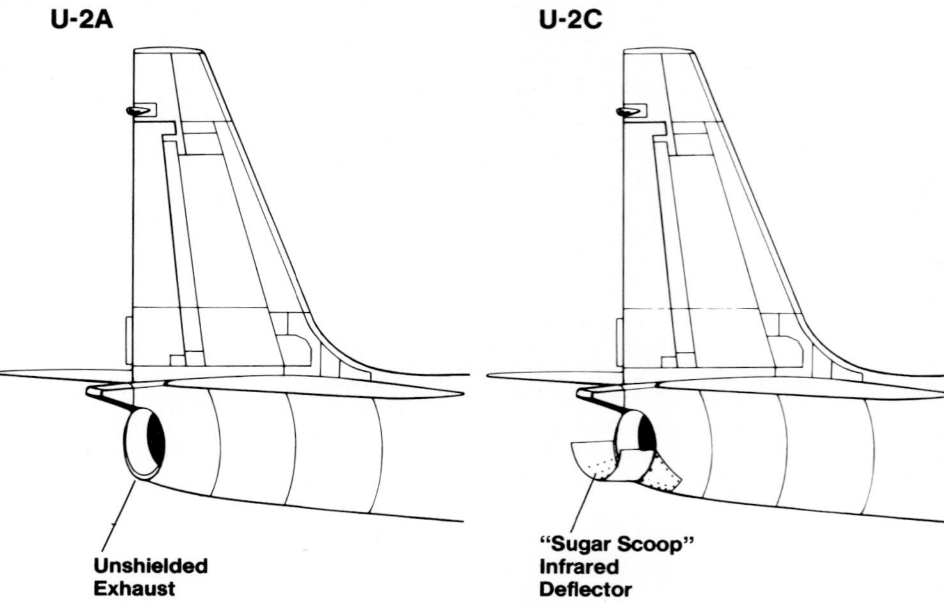

The short scoop shaped fairing under the exhaust of this U-2C is the "Sugar scoop" infrared deflector designed to lower the U-2s infrared signature and shield the aircraft from infrared homing air to air missiles fired from below.

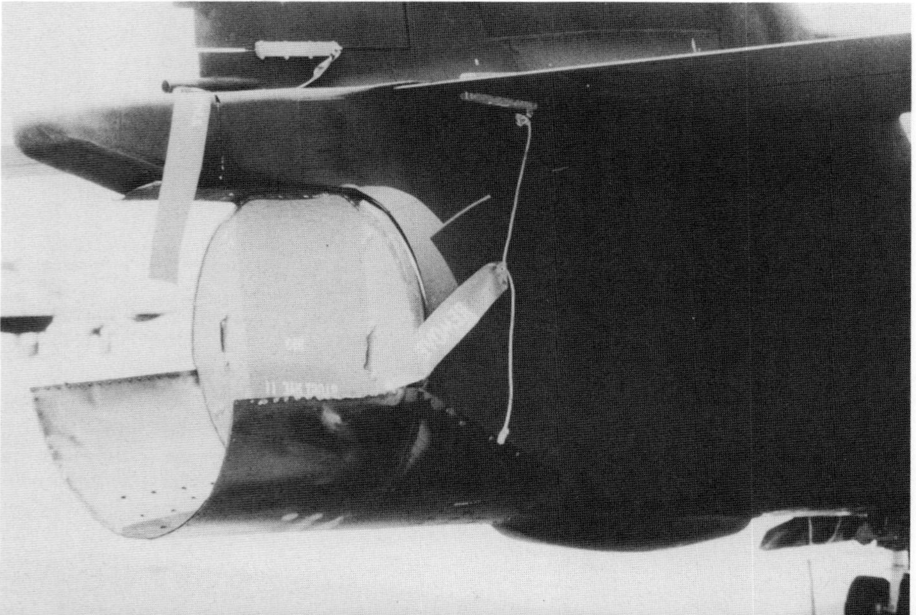

This natural metal and Flat Black U-2D of the Edwards Flight Test Center has a large sensor housing over the second cockpit. The U-2D carried the second crew member in a cockpit installed in the modified Q-Bay. (LAC)

This overall Gloss White U-2CT of the 100th SRW carries 1976 BiCentennial markings on the tail. The SAC fuselage band is Blue with White stars, while the shield on the tail is Light Blue with two US flags in the center. This U-2CT was built from the airframes of several crashed U-2As. (Roth)

Cockpit Development

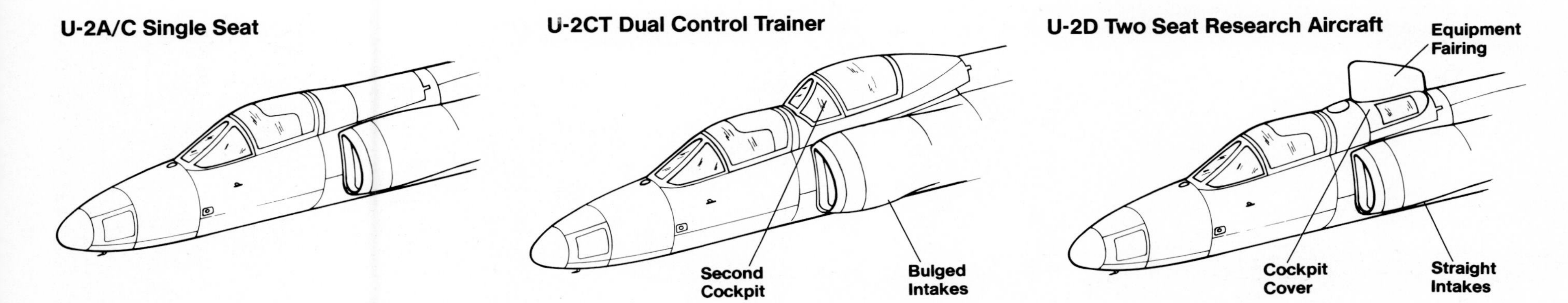

The "bullseyes" painted on the tail and upper wing of this Edwards AFB based U-2D are for focusing cameras carried on board the chase aircraft during tests. (Besecker via Andrews)

The rear cockpit canopy on the U-2D was hinged at the rear and opened upward. This U-2D has been modified with a large air scoop, called a "pickle barrel", between the cockpits. The U-2D was not configured with dual controls and was used for various high altitude research missions. (USAF via Andrews)

The cockpit of a U-2C is painted in Cockpit Gray. The fan attached to the canopy kept the canopy glass from fogging at high altitudes. The large circular screen above the control wheel is the pilots drift sight which gave the pilot a panoramic view below the aircraft. (LAC)

Later U-2D (56-6721) had the rear cockpit cover modified and was re-painted in the Flight Test Center paint scheme of overall Gloss White with Red stripes. The wing support stands under the extreme outer wing panels keep the weight of the aircraft off of the pogos when the aircraft was parked for long periods. (LAC)

This overall Light Gray U-2F has been fitted with Rams Horn SIGINT (Signals Intelligence) collection antennas on the upper rear fuselage and has a shortened dorsal electronics canoe. (100th SRW)

Air Refueling Receptacle

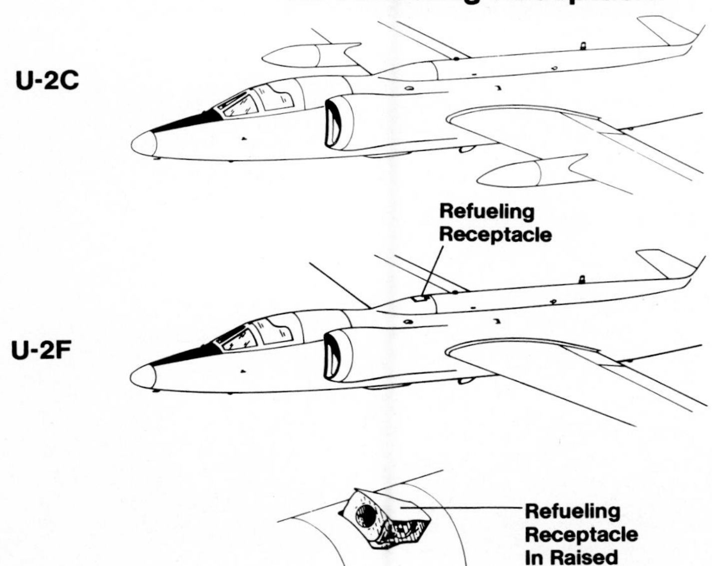

CIA Operations

While the Skunk Works was building the first production aircraft, the CIA was selecting and training aircrews. To pass the CIA screening process pilots had to demonstrate endurance, resistance to claustrophobia, and had to be cleared for high level security clearances. The pilots were ex-military, or military pilots that volunteered and were "transferred" to the CIA from their respective service. Various covers were used and a number of these pilots were "employed" by Lockheed under the title "Flight Test Consultants." Before beginning flight training, these crews were trained and briefed on CIA operations and regulations — which they found were far more rigid than any military regulations. By April of 1956 the first group of flight crews had completed their CIA indoctrination, U-2 flight training, and were declared operationally ready. The crews, along with the first two production U-2As, were flown by C-124 Globemaster cargo aircraft to RAF Lakenheath, England to begin preparations for their first operational mission. To preserve security, the unit was given a military cover designation, Weather Reconnaissance Squadron (Provisional) -1 and a cover story of being a high altitude weather research unit.

Nearly a year earlier, in July of 1955, President Eisenhower had proposed an "Open Skies" policy for the entire world — including the Soviet Union. It was known that the Soviets had a nuclear capability and were developing a delivery system capable of intercontinental strikes. Since most US Government activities are open to the public, Eisenhower was willing to let the world watch — if we could do the same. Nikita Kruschev and the Soviet leadership balked at the proposal and refused to negotiate on it. With the Soviet refusal to negotiate, Operation OVERFLIGHT, the clandestine aerial surveillance of the Soviet Union, was given the go-ahead.

With the handful of CIA pilots and U-2s in position at RAF Lakenheath, President Eisenhower gave permission for the first overflights of Soviet airspace. High-ranking British officials, however, who had been briefed on the true mission of the "weather aircraft" and the possible consequences, objected to having the overflights originate from British soil. As a result WRS(P)-1 moved to Wiesbaden, West Germany and it was from this base that the first overflight took place.

On 4 July 1956, Article 347 (U-2A Air Force serial 56-6680) left Wiesbaden AB bound for Moscow and Leningrad, two of the most heavily defended areas in the world. The flight was a complete success and Soviet defenses had been caught off guard. The Soviets made no mention of the intruder aircraft to the world press, and the photographs obtained by the U-2 proved to be phenomenally clear. Additional overflights were scheduled and received President Eisenhower's immediate approval.

The second CIA unit, WRS(P)-2, became operational at Incirlik AB, near Adana, Turkey in August of 1956. Officially known as WRS(P)-2, the unit's CIA designation was Detachment 10-10. In February of 1957 WRS(P)-1 moved to Giebelstadt AB, a remote base near Wurzburg, Germany. During mid-1957, WRS(P)-1 was consolidated with WRS(P)-2 with both units moving to Incirlik after it was discovered that Giebelstadt had been penetrated by Soviet intelligence — the KGB. Overflights continued into 1960, with over thirty missions being flown, all with prior Presidential approval. Missions penetrated deep into Russian airspace, taking off from Turkish bases and returning to the same base some nine hours later. During 1958 a third unit, WRS(P)-3, became operational at Atsugi Air Base in Japan for overflights of Asian targets.

The Soviet air defense force, the PVO, made a number of attempts to intercept these early overflights, although all were unsuccessful. The MiG-15, MiG-17 and MiG-19 interceptors then in service could not reach the U-2's operating altitude. Later MiG-21 fighters would be used to attempt zoom climb intercepts, and although the MiG-21 could reach the U-2's altitude in a perfectly executed zoom climb, it could not maneuver. At the apex of the climb the MiG-21 was ballistic and U-2 pilots could simply turn away from

This CIA U-2B is equipped with an electronics fairing on the fuselage spine, and a "sugar scoop" infrared deflector on the underside of the tailpipe. CIA U-2s involved in over flights of hostile territory were painted overall Flat Black as camouflage against the Black sky at 60,000 feet. (LAC)

With a starter unit in place, this CIA U-2B prepares for another mission. The hump on the fuselage spine is a full length electronics housing. Although operated by the CIA, the aircraft were usually maintained by Air Force personnel. (CIA via Andrews)

A CIA U-2 rolls out after returning from a successful mission. The U-2 would drag the heavy wing during landing if the fuel load was not properly balanced and during approach pilots transferred fuel from one wing to the other to balance the aircraft. (LAC)

Power's Flight 1 May 1960

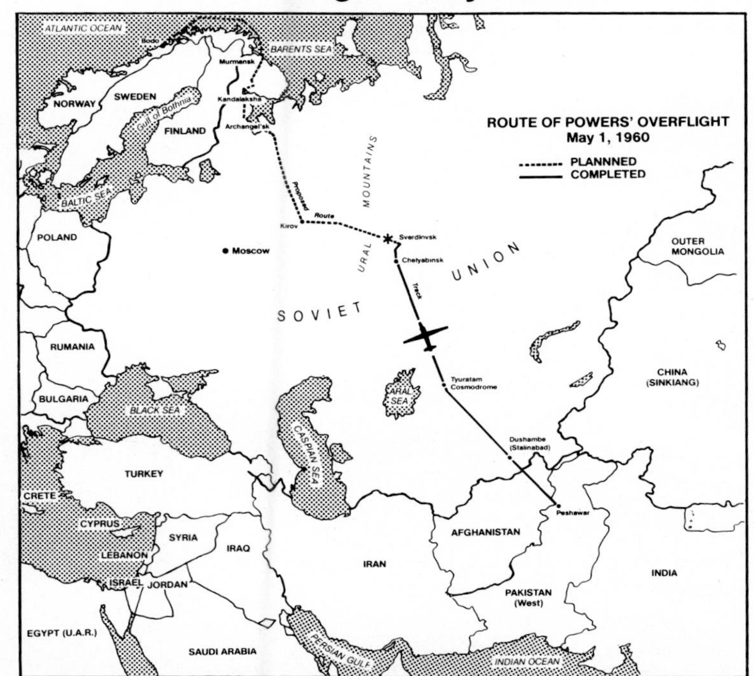

Kelly Johnson examines the photographs released by the Soviets that were claimed to be the U-2 flown by Francis Gary Powers after he was shot down on 1 May 1960. After careful examination of the photographs, Johnson stated that the aircraft was not a U-2. Later photographs enabled Johnson to determine that the U-2 had lost its wings in flight. (LAC via Andrews)

the MiG and avoid interception. The control surfaces on the AA-2 Atoll air-to-air missiles carried by the MiG-21 were too small to allow the missile to maneuver at altitude and they too went ballistic and could not guide on the U-2.

Conventional anti-aircraft artillery was completely ineffectual and the Soviet air defense planners turned to the developing technology of the surface-to-air missile (SAM) as their best chance to destroy the intruders. It was the U-2 more than any other aircraft, that led to the rapid development and operational deployment of the Soviet SA-2 Guideline missile, the infamous SAM of the Vietnam War. All U-2 combat losses have been credited to SAMs — including Francis Gary Powers in 1960.

Francis Gary Powers had been a US Air Force 1st Lieutenant and F-84G Thunderjet pilot before "resigning" from the Air Force in April of 1956 to become a CIA pilot. He was a member of the second group of Agency pilots trained at The Ranch graduating in May of 1956. Powers was sent to Incirlik AB, Turkey as part of Det10-10, flying his first mission, a border electronic surveillance mission, in September of 1956. On 1 May 1960, International Labor Day, he took off on his twenty-eighth (and last) mission. The mission was scheduled to be the first overflight to go completely across the Soviet Union.

His mission objective was to photograph the Intercontinental Ballistic Missile sites at Plesetsk and Sverlovsk. At 0626, Powers started his takeoff roll in Article 360 (AF serial 56-6693). The route the U-2 was to take would go from Peshawar AB, Turkey, northwest over Afghanistan crossing the Soviet border near Dushambe (ex-Stalinabad). The flight would than proceed across Soviet territory to the missile site at Sverlovsk, then west to Kirov, and northwest to Murmansk where the aircraft would exit Soviet airspace. The flight would proceed over the Barents Sea, around Finland and Sweden, finally landing at Bodo, Norway — a total distance of 3,800 miles with a nine hour flight time.

In his book "Operation Overflight", Powers recalled that everything was routine until reaching Sverdlovsk. Unknown to Powers, the Soviet air defense forces were ready and had planned to destroy the U-2 at all costs. A number of MiG-19 fighters would attempt zoom climb intercepts while SA-2 SAM missile site radars tracked the U-2 and prepared to launch their missiles at the best possible moment. According to Soviet sources, some fourteen SA-2s were simultaneously launched at the U-2, exploding at the same time near Powers' aircraft. The lightly constructed and fragile U-2 was over stressed by the shock waves and the fuselage failed somewhere near the tail. Powers bailed out of the crippled U-2 and was captured immediately upon landing. One of the MiG-19s engaged in the intercept attempt was also shot down by an SA-2.

The Soviets had gained a propaganda coup of enormous proportions. They had shot down and captured a US pilot during a spy flight over the Soviet Union and were quick to make the most of it parading Powers before the world press. Both the Pentagon and US public wanted quick answers to what had gone wrong. After studying photos of the downed U-2, Kelly Johnson deduced that the wings had separated from the fuselage because of 'down-bending' as a result of the violent upward thrust of the SAM shock wave. In later talks with Powers, then a Lockheed employee, Johnson concluded that the SAM attack had knocked off the right horizontal stabilizer, causing the U-2 to snap over onto its back, overstressing the wings and causing their failure. The Soviets placed Powers on public trial as a spy, where he was convicted and sentenced to ten years in the Lubyanka Prison at Moscow. One year, nine months, and ten days later, Powers was exchanged for Soviet KGB agent Rudolf Abel who had been captured by the FBI in 1958.

The political fallout from the Powers shootdown was tremendous. The Summit Meeting that had been scheduled for 16 May was cancelled. The U-2's mission had been to obtain photographs of the Soviet ICBM sites, which Eisenhower would use at the Summit as evidence of the Soviet military buildup. After the Summit was cancelled all future overflights of Soviet territory were curtailed. U-2 bases were closed down and the units transferred back to the United States. After the Powers incident the CIA slowly shifted all U-2 operations and aircraft to the Air Force.

Kelly Johnson and Francis Gary Powers discuss his fateful mission following Power's release from a Soviet prison. Powers was killed in August of 1977 while flying a traffic helicopter for a Los Angeles TV station. (LAC)

A Central Intelligence Agency U-2B over Southern California. This aircraft eventually was lost over South Vietnam on 8 October 1966 — the only U-2 lost in the Vietnam War. (CIA via Andrews)

Air Force U-2 Operations

The Air Force received its first U-2 on 11 July 1957 when the aircraft was handed over to the 4080th Strategic Reconnaissance Wing, 4028th SRS, Strategic Air Command at Laughlin AFB, Texas. The unit's stated mission was weather reconnaissance and high altitude air sampling (HASP). These missions were flown to detect and obtain samples of radioactive fallout in the atmosphere from atomic surface detonations that were taking place around the globe. These samples could be studied to determine a number of important factors about the weapons being tested. In addition to the HASP mission the 4028th SRS flew U-2 photographic reconnaissance missions, particularly over the island of Cuba.

Both CIA and Air Force U-2s had been monitoring Cuba since Fidel Castro had come to power and openly declared himself a Marxist. On 29 August 1962, a CIA U-2 pilot brought back the first indications that a Soviet military buildup was taking place on the island. SA-2 Guideline SAM sites were spotted along with indications that ballistic missile sites were being prepared. President Kennedy ordered the overflights increased and Air Force pilots were brought into the CIA detachment at McCoy AFB, Florida. Intelligence agents inside Cuba had reported seeing several large cylindrical objects being off-loaded from Soviet freighters and missions were scheduled to confirm the presence of these suspected missiles.

On 14 October 1962, MAJ Steve Heyser, flying a CIA-operated U-2E overflew Cuba at over 70,000 feet. The photos he took shook the entire world and brought the United States and the Soviet Union to the brink of World War 3. Heyser's photos proved unquestionably that the Soviets had introduced medium range ballistic missiles to the island and that missile launch sites were only weeks away from being fully operational. These photos were the beginning of the Cuban Missile Crisis.

President Kennedy ordered an immediate naval quarantine of Cuba, sealing the island nation from all incoming shipping. Additionally he informed the world that "a missile launched against the United States from Cuba would be regarded as an attack by the Soviet Union and we would retaliate in kind". Kennedy demanded that the missile threat be removed from Cuba and to verify Soviet actions U-2 and other reconnaissance flights over Cuba were increased, with U-2s of the 4080th SRW performing a major portion of these overflights. 4080th crews overflew Cuba 102 times between 14 October and 16 December 1962, with three U-2s and their pilots being lost. Major Rudolph Andersen was shot down by an SA-2 Guideline missile and two other U-2s were lost due to unknown causes. For their actions during the Crisis, the 4080th SRW was awarded their second Outstanding Unit Award.

During 1963 Air Force U-2s were assigned to the High Altitude Clear Air Turbulance Program (HICAT) which conducted a series of flights to investigate the phenomenon of high altitude clear air turbulance. At least one U-2 of the 6512th Test Group, the *Smokey Joes*, based at Edwards Air Force Base was modified with highly sensitive measuring equipment carried on a long boom mounted under the nose. The boom carried vanes for measuring air pressure, vertical and lateral wind gusts, and fluctuating air velocities. The project lasted several years and the uniquely painted U-2 was deployed to a number of locations including; Puerto Rico, Alaska, Australia, Fuji, New Zealand, and Panama. Data obtained from these tests was instrumental in the design of future high altitude supersonic aircraft, including the British/French SST transport, the Concorde.

Beginning in late 1963 U-2s of the 4080th SRW were active in operations over North Vietnam under the code name *Lucky Dragon* (later changed to *Trojan Horse* and finally *Giant Dragon*). These overflights continued until North Vietnamese air defenses were upgraded with the SA-2 Guideline missiles. The presence of SA-2s in North Vietnam caused the U-2 flights to be cancelled since they were now considered too dangerous. With the withdrawal of the U-2 from North Vietnamese overflights, Lightning Bug remotely piloted vehicles (RPVs or drones) and Air Force high speed reconnaissance

With the "Howdah" sunshield secured in place this U-2A of the Edwards Flight Test Center rests on the ramp at Edwards Air Force base. Edwards U-2s were used for a variety of test missions and were some of the last U-2As to remain in service. (USAF via Andrews)

aircraft such as the RF-4C Phantom took over the reconnaissance duties over the North. The U-2s, however, were still used for stand off surveillance missions. One aircraft was lost during the Vietnam War, a U-2C (56-6690) which was lost over South Vietnam from structural failure.

Following the Vietnam War, detachments of U-2s were assigned to various bases throughout the Free World, flying standoff border electronic surveillance missions. In 1975 six U-2Cs were deployed to Europe to test a prototype targeting system under the code name *Pave Onyx*. Three U-2s flying at precisely known distances were used to triangulate the locations of Warsaw Pact electronic emitters while flying over friendly airspace. At the specific request of the British government, these six U-2Cs were painted in a special two tone Gray camouflage, known as the *Sabre Scheme*, instead of their standard Flat Black scheme. The U-2s remained at RAF Wethersfield until August of 1975, when they were ferried back to Davis Monthan AFB.

The threat from surface to air missiles had ended high altitude U-2 overflights of hostile territory with that mission now being carried out by ultra-sophisticated reconnaissance satellites and ultra-high speed high altitude aircraft such as the Kelly Johnson-designed SR-71A Blackbird. U-2s, however, continued to serve in research projects, standoff surveillance, and a number of civil disaster relief missions. During the late 1970s non-military flights became increasingly more prevalent. During one such flight, several U-2s were used to conduct at least two ten and a half hour missions from California to Guatamala to survey the damage caused by an earthquake which devastated Guatamala City during February of 1976. Another Air Force U-2 was used to photograph a 600 square mile area of the Pacific searching for survivors of a sunken ketch. Flying from 60,000 feet, the U-2s cameras detected the ship's yellow life raft and the survivors were successfully rescued.

HASP WU-2As were operated by a detachment of the 4080th SRW based at RAAF Laverton for missions over the Pacific to measure radiation levels from French and Chinese atomic tests. This WU-2A has had the flight control surfaces replaced with those from an overall Black U-2. (AFM)

This overall Light Gray (FS 36473) U-2A of the 4080th SRW is equipped with "slipper" type fuel tanks on the wing leading edges and a small electronics fairing on the fuselage spine. This aircraft (56-6953) was originally built as a U-2D, and later converted back to U-2A standards. (USAF via Andrews)

Air Force ground crews tow a WU-2A from its hanger at RAAF Laverton, Australia. This aircraft was later one of ten U-2s used for surveillance overflights of Cuba during the 1962 Cuban Missile Crisis. (Andrews)

U-2D 56-6722 was later reconfigured with the second cockpit and upper fuselage sensor fairing replaced by a short electronics canoe on the fuselage spine. The aircraft is painted overall Flat Black with White letters, while the sensor boom on the nose was striped in Red and White. (AFM)

This overall Flat Black U-2D of the Edwards Flight Test Center was modified for use in the High Altitude Clear Air Turbulence (HICAT) program. The aircraft was fitted with a long sensor probe under the nose, which was painted with Red and White stripes. (LAC)

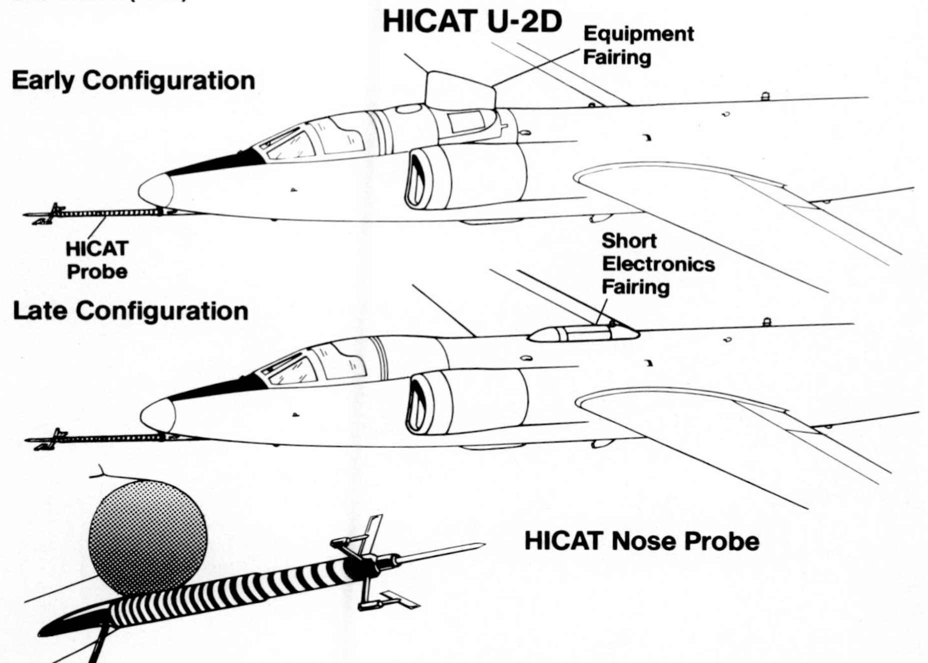

Three Air Force ground crewmen ride the wing of a HICAT U-2D (56-6722) to keep it balanced on the pogo after landing. It was normal practice for one of the ground crew to insert at least one of the pogos while the aircraft was on landing rollout. (LAC)

U-2D 56-6722 was acquired by the Air Force Museum at Wright Patterson Air Force Base in Dayton, Ohio. The aircraft was reconfigured to U-2A standards and repainted overall Black with Red serials as it would have appeared during operational service. (Dave Menard)

A pair of U-2s enter the landing pattern at Edwards Air Force Base. The U-2D (56-6722) in the foreground was assigned to the 6512th Test Group and carries a Black chevron with the Edwards Flight Test Center crest and a "Smoky Joe" cartoon on the tail.(LAC)

An Air Force ground crewman removes the Q-Bay hatch from an Edwards AFB Flight Test Center U-2D. The bulged area on the fuselage spine is the cockpit cover for the second cockpit. The canvas cover on the "pickle barrel" air sampling intake has a pair of eyes painted on it. (Jacobs via Andrews)

Three Flight Test Center U-2s in formation prior to tests of the satellite recovery system. The lead aircraft, a U-2D (56-6722) carries two dummy satellites in the Q-Bay, which were ejected near 70,000 feet. An HC-130 recovery aircraft would then track, intercept, and recover the descending satellite. (AFM)

An overall Light Gray WU-2A (56-6696) of the 4080th SRW assigned to the High Altitude Sampling Program (HASP) in Australia during 1963.

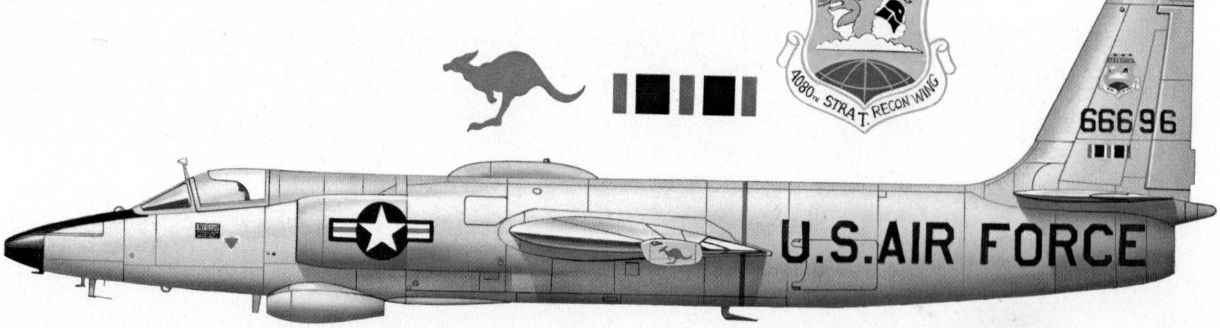

A CIA U-2B configured for Electronic Intelligence (ELINT) missions during the mid-1960s.

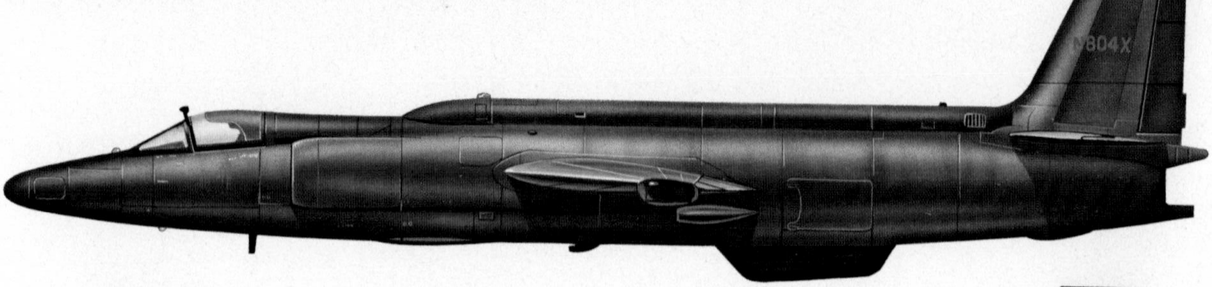

A natural metal U-2A (56-6701) of the 6512th Test Group at Edwards AFB, California during the late 1950s.

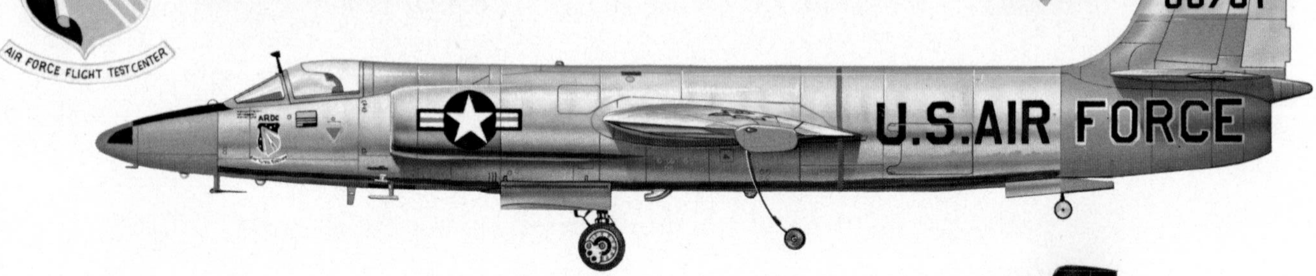

An overall Flat Black U-2F (56-6707) of the 4080th Strategic Reconnaissance Wing detachment at Operating Location-20, Bien Hoa Air Base, Vietnam during 1965.

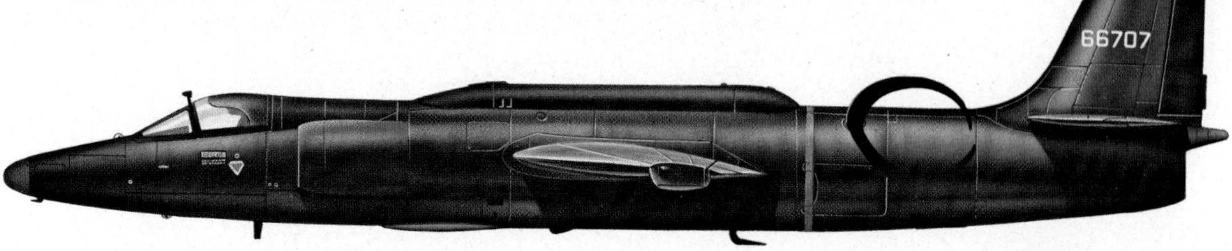

This U-2D (56-6722) assigned to Project HICAT, carries a White Polar Bear and Red Kangaroo markings from its deployments to Alaska and Australia during the early 1960s.

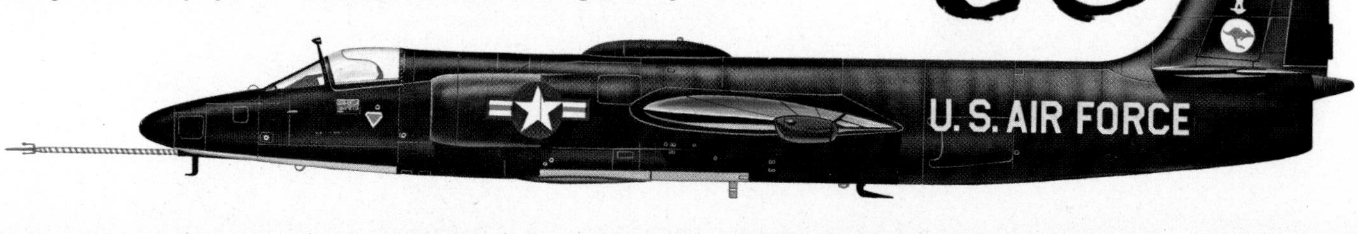

nia during 1973. This aircraft was formerly Air Force 56-6681.

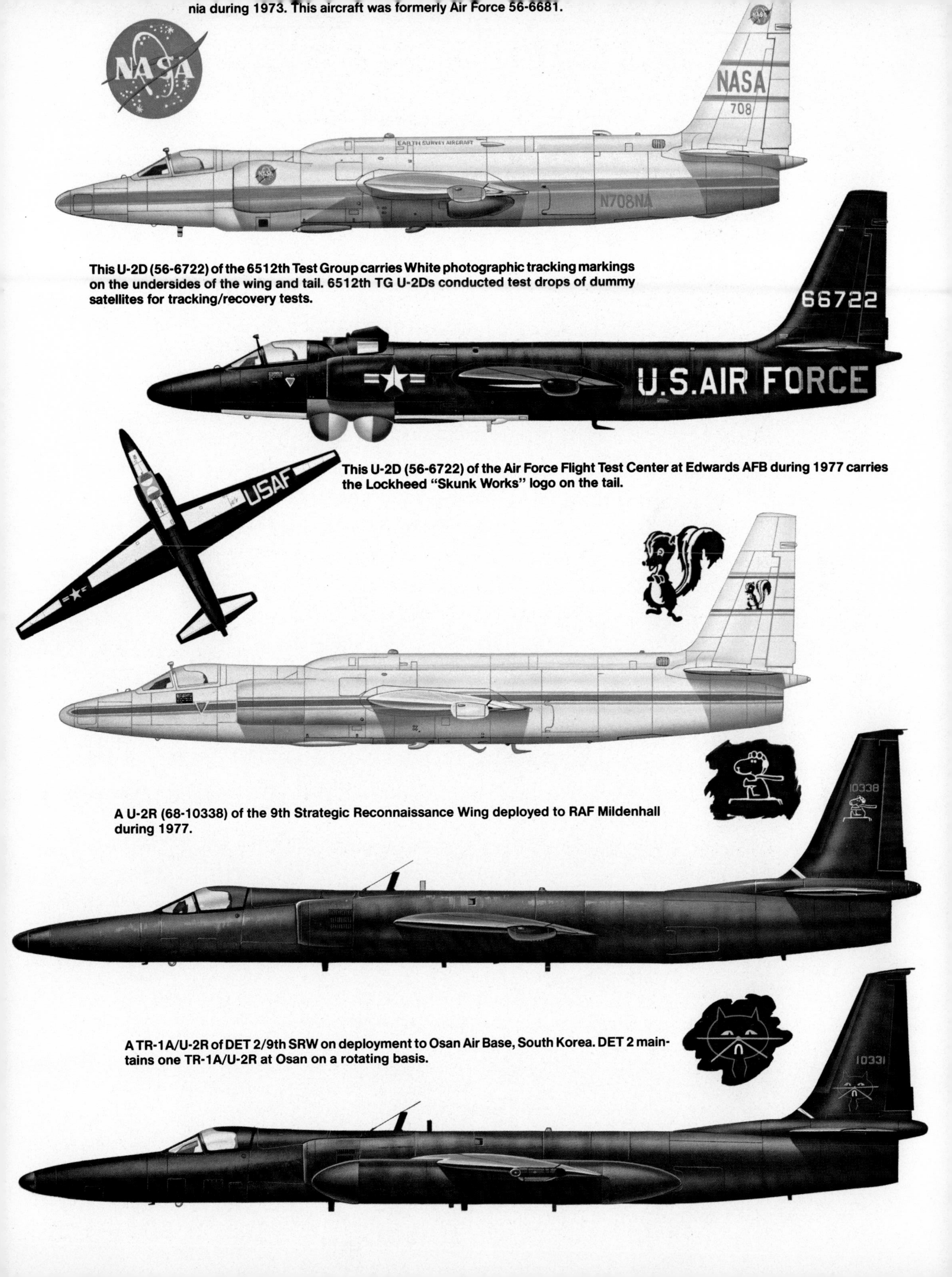

This U-2D (56-6722) of the 6512th Test Group carries White photographic tracking markings on the undersides of the wing and tail. 6512th TG U-2Ds conducted test drops of dummy satellites for tracking/recovery tests.

This U-2D (56-6722) of the Air Force Flight Test Center at Edwards AFB during 1977 carries the Lockheed "Skunk Works" logo on the tail.

A U-2R (68-10338) of the 9th Strategic Reconnaissance Wing deployed to RAF Mildenhall during 1977.

A TR-1A/U-2R of DET 2/9th SRW on deployment to Osan Air Base, South Korea. DET 2 maintains one TR-1A/U-2R at Osan on a rotating basis.

This Light Gray over Flat Black U-2A is prepared for movement at Edwards Air Force Base during 1962 mounted on a specially designed transport dolly. The ground handling dolly simplified movement of the U-2 on the ground, since the aircraft did not taxi well. (USAF via Andrews)

This U-2A is painted with White photo-tracking markings on the undersides of the wings. A number of U-2 were painted in this manner to increase visibility to ground tracking stations during various test missions. (LAC)

A U-2A (56-6721) following conversion to the U-2D configuration carries classified sensors on the upper fuselage and in the Q-Bay, with a special electronics fairing just visible behind the second cockpit. The White markings are for photo-tracking from ground stations. (Muir)

A U-2C (56-6952) on the ramp at Operating Location (OL) 20 — Bien Hoa AB, South Vietnam. The 4080th SRW deployed a detachment of U-2s to OL-20 in the Spring of 1964 under the code name Operation DRAGON LADY. (100th SRW)

This U-2F (56-6707) at OL-20 during the mid-1960s is equipped with "rams horns" antennas for SIGINT/COMINT missions and an air refueling receptacle on the forward portion of the canoe. SIGINT and COMINT missions involved interception of North Vietnamese and Viet Cong radio signals and communications traffic. (100th SRW)

This U-2C of the 100th SRW at Davis-Monthan AFB in March of 1975 is one of six aircraft that were re-painted the two-tone Gray "Saber Scheme" camouflage at the request of the British government prior to their deployment to English bases. (Roth)

This "Saber Scheme" U-2C (56-6692) carried special sensors as part of the *Pave Onyx* program to monitor Soviet radar emissions while flying over friendly airspace. The fairing on the trailing edge of the starboard wing is a Radar Homing and Warning (RHAW) antenna. (LAC)

U-2R

By early 1966 the number of remaining U-2s in the inventories of both the CIA and US Air Force had been significantly reduced through combat losses and attrition. To make up for these losses the Defense Department, acting for both the CIA and Air Force, awarded Lockheed a development/production contract for one prototype and twelve production aircraft in August of 1966. Rather than just reestablish the original U-2 production facility, the CIA approached Lockheed with a proposal to redesign the U-2 to correct some of the deficiencies in the original U-2A. As sensor packages had increased in weight, the original U-2 began suffering from poor flight characteristics at mission altitudes. The CIA wanted this problem corrected in the new U-2 production program along with improvements in the landing characteristics, cramped cockpit, range, and payload capabilities of the aircraft. Additionally the CIA wanted the airframe strengthened to improve the aircraft's fatigue life. Kelly Johnson's Skunk Works team began work on correcting the problem areas and came up with a design that, while based on the U-2A, was an entirely new aircraft.

Lockheed began work on the U-2R (R for Revised) prototype in late 1966. The 17,000 lbst Pratt & Whitney J75-P-13B of the earlier U-2C series was retained for the U-2R since the engine was reliable and would provide sufficient power for the new design. The fuselage was stretched both in front and behind the wing increasing overall length from 49.7 feet to 62.7 feet. The fuselage stretch allowed room for an enlarged cockpit with a zero-zero ejection seat, an enlarged "Q" bay capable of housing updated sensor payloads, electronic countermeasures systems, a lengthened jet tailpipe to reduce infrared emissions, and provisions for an optional arresting hook for carrier operations.

The horizontal and vertical tail surfaces were both enlarged (the horizontal surfaces of late production U-2Rs have been reinforced with external ribs running back from the stabilizer leading edge). The wing was increased in length from 80.17 feet to 103 feet. The lengthened wing featured retractable leading edge stall strips and wing spoilers to improve low speed control during landing, enlarged fuel tanks, and folding wingtips for carrier operations. Additionally the wing was strengthened to permit the use of larger wing mounted sensor or fuel "super pods" which attached to the wing leading edge. These structural changes raised the gross weight from 24,000 pounds (U-2C) to 41,000 pounds for the U-2R. To handle the increased weight the main landing gear was strengthened.

Performance differed little from the earlier U-2A series except in range. With an additional 1,700 gallons of internal fuel, range was increased from 4,700 miles (U-2C) to over 6,200 miles for the U-2R. Service U-2Rs have flown non-stop from Beale AFB, California, to forward bases in England — a distance of some 5,600 miles with a flight time of some fourteen hours.

The prototype U-2R made its first flight on 28 August 1967. After a short and intensive flight test period, the first production U-2Rs were delivered to the CIA at Edwards AFB, North Base, during late 1968. North Base had become the main CIA U-2 operating base following the stand down after the Powers incident. CIA U-2Rs were dispatched from North Base to Operating Locations (OLs) in Florida (for Cuban overflights) and Taiwan (for mainland China overflights).

Central Intelligence Agency aircraft, bearing Nationalist Chinese Air Force insignia and flown by Chinese crews, were used to overfly mainland China from 1968 through 1974. During 1974, however, all Chinese overflight operations were ordered cancelled in accordance with an agreement reached between the US and Red China following President Nixon's 1974 visit to China. Following the phaseout of the Chinese program CIA U-2 operations began a steady decline with the remaining Agency aircraft being passed to Air Force control.

During 1966 the Air Force had begun redesignating and relocating their U-2 units. The 4080th SRW, veteran of the Cuban Missile Crisis, moved from Laughlin AFB, Texas

The U-2R (R for Revised) eliminated many of the difficulties of the earlier U-2A. The U-2R has improved landing characteristics, greater range, and can carry a variety of updated sensors and ECM equipment. (LAC)

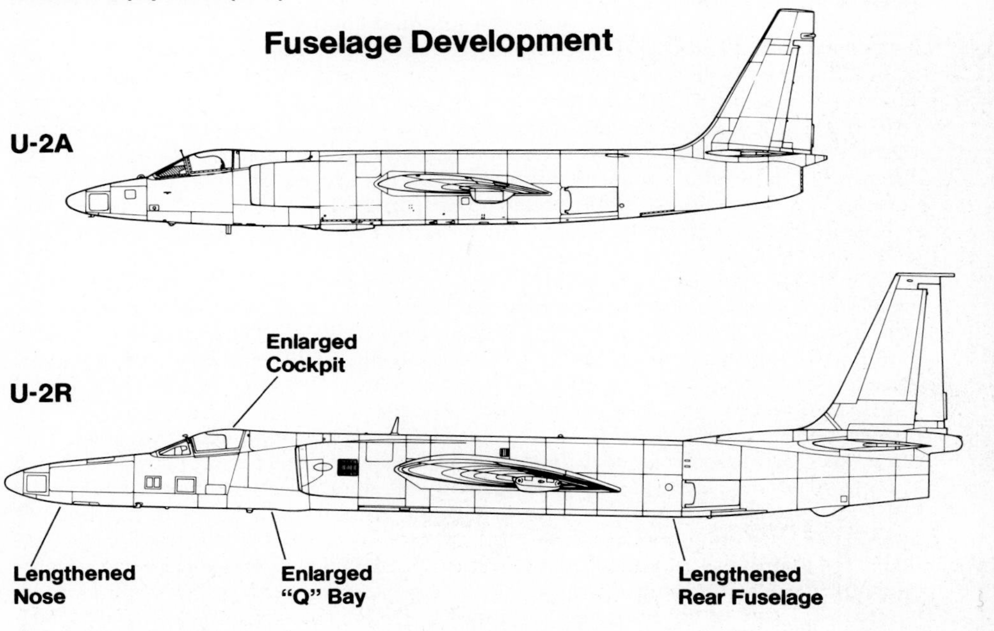

to Davis Monthan AFB, being redesignated the 100th SRW. During 1976 the Air Force elected to consolidate its strategic reconnaissance systems under one organization and the 100th SRW was transferred to Beale AFB, California. The consolidation placed the U-2 units within 9th SRW, alongside Lockheed's other reconnaissance platform — the SR-71A Blackbird.*

On the other side of the world, the Air Force U-2 detachment at OL-20 (Bien Hoa, Vietnam) had been brought up to full squadron strength during 1968 receiving the designation 99th SRS. The unit was later transferred to U-Tapao, Thailand during July of 1970 where it was involved with both pre and post strike reconnaissance missions in support of Operation LINEBACKER II (under the code name *Olympic Torch*). While in Thailand the squadron was also involved with missions aimed at monitoring Chinese communications under the code name *Senior Book*. The reliability of the U-2R enabled the squadron to set a number of new records for U-2 operations. Over 600 flight hours were flown during December of 1974, a total never before reached by a U-2 unit. With the end of the Vietnam war, the 99th SRS left Thailand in December of 1974, and its aircraft and crews were dispersed to detachments serving at a number of OLs in various parts of the world. Under the Air Force consolidation program during the Fall of 1976, it was decided that the U-2 contingent of the 9th SRW would retain the squadron designator, 99th SRS, with all Air Force U-2 assets being transferred to the 99th (the other U-2 unit designators, the 4080th and 100th were re-assigned to KC-135 units at Beale).

U-2EP-X

The U-2EP-X (Electronic Patrol-Experimental) was a modified U-2R used by the US Navy to test the suitability of the U-2R for aircraft carrier operations. Two aircraft were loaned to the Navy from the CIA during 1969 to conduct a series of carrier qualification tests aboard USS AMERICA off the Virginia coast. Lockheed test pilot Bill Park made a number of carrier landings and takeoffs during the three day carrier qualifications of the U-2R with the first landing being made on 21 November 1969. Test pilot Park reported that the U-2R was stable in the approach and had good wave off characteristics. He further stated that a 20 knot wind over the deck and the low approach speed of the U-2R would allow the U-2R to safely operate from carrier decks without an arresting hook. Takeoffs were made without using the carrier's catapults, since the high thrust to weight ratio and the lift generated by the 20 knot wind over the deck allowed the U-2R to takeoff with a deck run of under 300 feet. The test aircraft required no special modifications, other than the installation of the tail hook. With the success of these trials, Lockheed developed a field modification package consisting of the tail hook, wing tip skid stabilizers, and cockpit controls for the tail hook. By using the field modification kit, any U-2R could be made carrier capable on short notice.

In addition to the carrier suitability tests, the Navy also experimented with the U-2R for a unique mission. Several electronic surveillance systems then under development were installed in the U-2R under the test designator U-2EP-X. These included a highly modified RCA X-band radar, AN/ALQ-110 Electronic Intelligence Receiver, and a forward looking infrared system. These systems were intended to allow the U-2 to patrol huge areas of ocean in the maritime reconnaissance role. One of the test aircraft was further modified with a AN/APS-116 forward looking radar mounted in the nose. This radar was specifically designed to detect submarine snorkel and periscopes. The forward looking infrared system was carried in specially developed slipper wing pods, while the AN/APS 110 and RCA X band radar were mounted in the "Q" bay with the antenna housed in a faired radome extending below the bay. The success of the test program led Lockheed to propose an armed version of the U-2EP-X which would carry the electro-optically guided Condor anti-ship missiles. This program, however, was not adopted. Upon completion of the test program both aircraft were converted back to standard U-2R configuration and returned to the CIA.

**For information on the SR-71 see Squadron/Signal #1055 "SR-71 Blackbird In Action".*

The upper fuselage of the U-2R reveals the blade UHF communications antenna, whip radio antenna, heat exchanger air outlet (behind the blade antenna), "Q" bay upper hatch (in front of antennas), oil cooler outlet on the engine air intakes and rear view mirror on the canopy framing. (LAC)

The rectangular boxes inside the main engine air intakes are the ram air intakes for the air conditioning system. The small glass dome on the underside of the nose is the periscope for the pilots drift sight and the rounded fairings on the sides of the air intakes are ECM antennas. (LAC)

The U-2R has a thirteen foot extension to the fuselage and an extended wing with a twenty-three foot greater wingspan than the U-2A series. This overall Flat Black U-2R (68-10339) is an early production aircraft. (LAC)

Resembling an astronaut, a U-2R pilot dressed in the S1010B pressure suit poses in front of an early production U-2R. The suit is completely pressurized and is cooled on the ground by the portable air conditioning unit carried by the pilot. This suit can only be worn in the more spacious U-2R/TR-1A cockpit. (LAC)

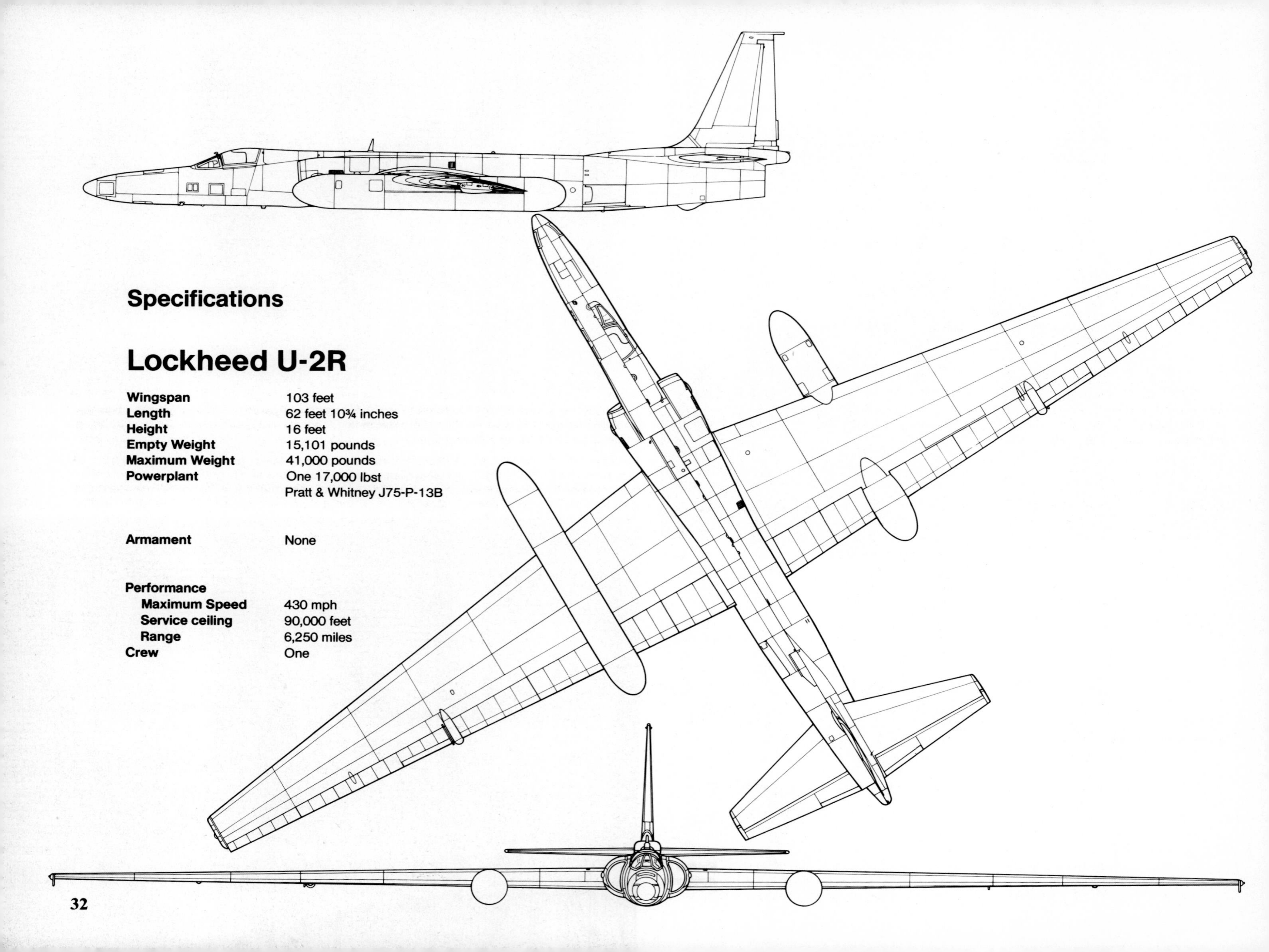

Specifications

Lockheed U-2R

Wingspan	103 feet
Length	62 feet 10¾ inches
Height	16 feet
Empty Weight	15,101 pounds
Maximum Weight	41,000 pounds
Powerplant	One 17,000 lbst Pratt & Whitney J75-P-13B
Armament	None
Performance	
Maximum Speed	430 mph
Service ceiling	90,000 feet
Range	6,250 miles
Crew	One

The wingtip skids of late production U-2Rs were equipped with RHAW antennas mounted at a 45 degree angle to the line of flight. These antennas provide side looking radar warning coverage as part of the U-2R defensive ECM system. (LAC)

Wing Skids

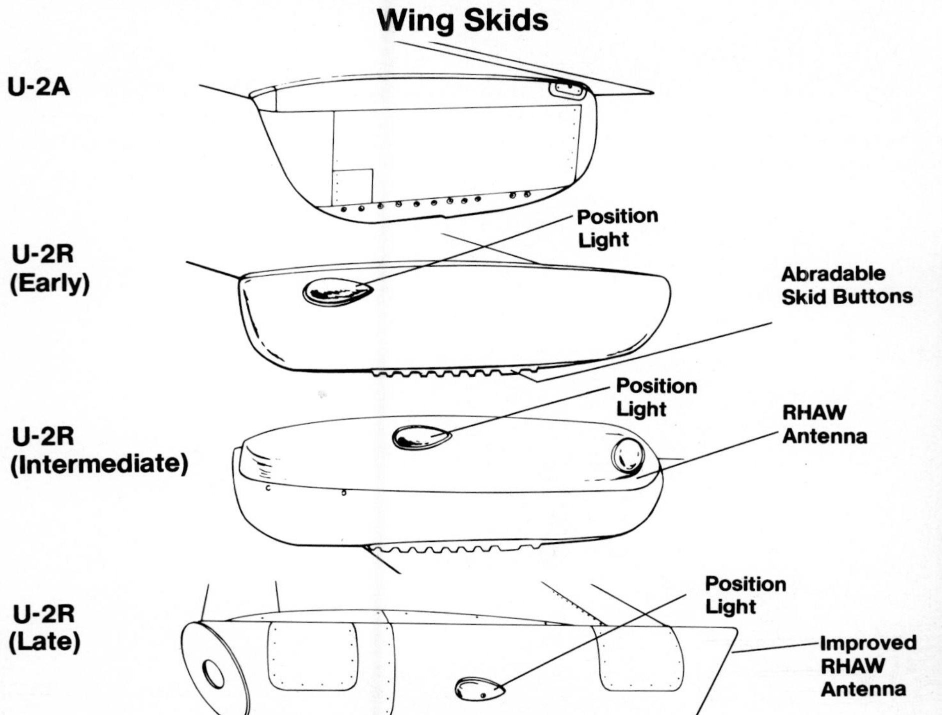

The CIA deployed U-2Rs to Taiwan for overflight missions against Red China. These missions were halted during 1974 following President Nixons visit to China. This U-2R carries small Nationalist Chinese Air Force insignia on the fuselage behind the open speed brake. (CIA via Andrews)

A U-2R (68-10339) of the 99th SRS, 9th SRW on the ramp at Beale AFB, California. This U-2R is equipped with intermediate type Radar Homing and Warning (RHAW) antennas on the wing skids. (Roth)

An ASARS equipped U-2R on final approach for landing at the Lockheed Palmdale facility. The TR-1A contract also covered production of at least ten U-2Rs to replenish the depleted Air Force U-2R inventory. (LAC)

A trio of variously configured U-2Rs of the 9th SRW on the ramp at Beale AFB. The aircraft in the center carries SIGINT/COMINT super pods in addition to the lengthened nose radome of an ASARS equipped aircraft. (LAC)

U-2Rs were delivered to the 99th SRS detachment at Bien Hoa during 1969, just prior to the unit's move to U-Tapao Air Base, Thailand. The U-2Rs were used extensively in support of Operation LINEBACKER II, the B-52 raids on Hanoi. (100 SRW)

Wing Pods

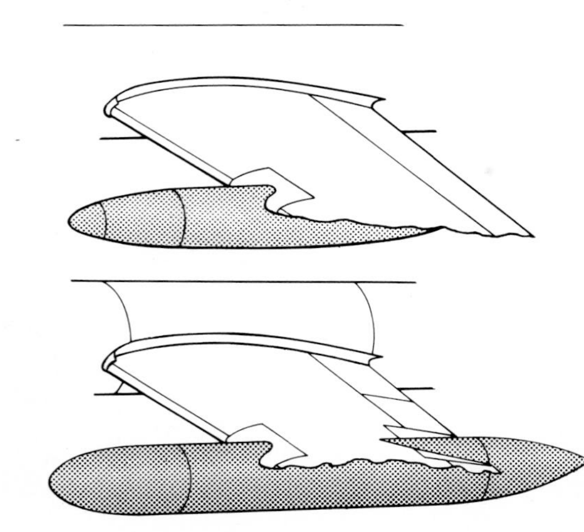

A long-nosed U-2R of the 9th SRW equipped with the Hughes Advanced Synthetic Aperture Radar System (ASARS) during one of the early system development flights. With the ASARS and Lockheed's Precision Emitter Location Strike System (PLSS), the U-2R can locate and identify radars over fifty miles away. (LAC)

Nose Modifications

U-2R

U-2R Advanced Synthetic Aperture Radar System

Antenna Fairings

Extended Nose ASARS Radome

U-2EP-X

Shortened Blunt Nose Radome

A U-2R in formation with a Gates Learjet during flight trials of new sensor equipment. This U-2R has the extended nose radome and sensor fairings associated with the Hughes Advanced Synthetic Aperture Radar System (ASARS) and carries side-looking airborne radar (SLAR) pods. (LAC)

This U-2R (68-10339) was modified for use by the Navy under the designation U-2EP-X (Electronics Patrol-Experimental). The nose radome was shortened and a pair of experimental Side Looking Airborne Radar (SLAR) sensor pods on the wings. At one point Lockheed proposed arming the U-2EP-X with Condor anti-ship missiles on underwing pylons. (LAC)

The Navy conducted carrier suitability trials with a CIA U-2R aboard USS AMERICA during 1969. The aircraft was fitted with an arrestor hook on the fuselage underside forward of the tail wheel, modified wingtip skids, and lift-dumping spoilers on the wings. (LAC)

U-2R Carrier Conversion

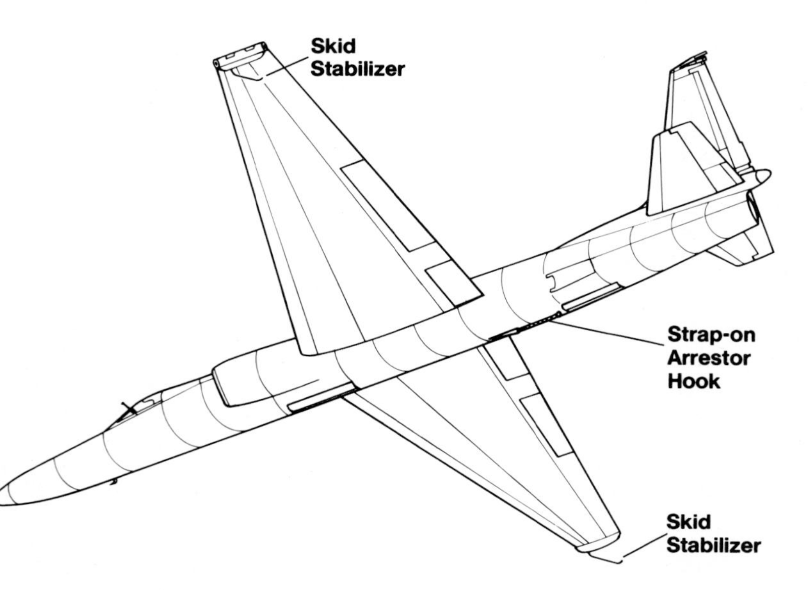

TR-1

By 1977 the active Air Force inventory of both early model U-2s and U-2Rs had been seriously reduced through accidents and attrition. This reduction came at a time when the Air Force saw an increasing need for the U-2R in standoff electronic surveillance, especially in the NATO theater. As a result, the Department of Defense awarded Lockheed a contract to re-open the U-2R production line. The initial portion of the contract, $10.2 million, was earmarked for refurbishing the U-2R production facility and producing whatever new tooling might be necessary.

On 16 November 1979, twelve years after the last U-2R had rolled off the Lockheed assembly line, production of the U-2R was reinstated. These new production aircraft were externally identical to the U-2R, with one exception. The Defense Department decided that the U-2 designation should be changed to one that more closely described the aircraft's mission. The production contract, issued in December of 1979, stated that the 'new' production U-2Rs would be built under the designation TR-1 (Tactical Reconnaissance-1).

The initial TR-1 production contract called for production of two TR-1As and one ER-2. The ER-2, or Earth Resources Two, is basically a TR-1A with all military systems deleted. The aircraft was built for the National Aeronautics and Space Administration (NASA) and is used for upper atmospheric research, alongside several U-2Cs that remain in the NASA inventory. Production of the TR-1A/ER-2 began in late 1979, with the first aircraft, the de-militarized ER-2, ready for testing on 11 May 1981. The prototype TR-1A followed the ER-2 off the production line making its first flight on 1 August 1981, followed shortly by the second TR-1A. These first two TR-1As were used for flight tests, systems development, and pilot training.

The TR-1A incorporated a number of minor internal changes from the U-2R and can carry the latest developments in airborne surveillance systems such as the Hughes Advanced Synthetic Aperture Radar System (ASARS) and Lockheed Precision Emitter Location Strike System (PLSS) pods, which had been tested and approved for use on the U-2R. The ASARS system is housed in a detachable bulbous lengthened nose radome and allows the TR-1 to see behind borders with a high resolution radar which is capable of producing imagery of hostile targets without exposing the TR-1 to hostile action. The PLSS system is a passive emitter-locator usually carried in a "Super pod" mounted on either wing. The system requires three TR-1s working together to triangulate hostile radar emitters. In a combat role these TR-1/U-2Rs would relay the information by real-time secure digital intelligence data link to a ground station where the location of the enemy radar is quickly plotted and a strike scheduled against it. These systems not only enhance the TR-1s ability to perform standoff surveillance, they are much lighter than previous systems and impose far fewer performance penalties.

Following a short flight test program the Air Force officially announced that Lockheed had been awarded a multi-phased production contract for the TR-1. Production would be spread over three years, with ten TR-1s being built in 1982, four in 1983, and five in 1984 with a total requirement for thirty-five aircraft (twenty-five TR-1s and ten U-2R attrition replacement aircraft) before production phased out. Included in the contract were two TR-1B two seat trainers. The TR-1B was similar to the earlier U-2CT with the second cockpit installed in the "Q" bay with a cockpit canopy installed above and to the rear of the pilot's cockpit. The first flight of the TR-1B took place on 23 February 1983.

In addition to the TR-1s, the contract also called for construction of ten U-2Rs as attrition replacements to fill out the depleted Air Force inventory. Additionally, an undisclosed portion of these aircraft were slated to meet the needs of "non-indigenous

The official rollout ceremony for the TR-1A took place at the Lockheed Palmdale, California facility. The rejuvenated U-2R/TR-1 production facility began deliveries of TR-1As in August of 1981, two months after the first flight of the NASA ER-2. (LAC)

The first production TR-1 was rolled out in August of 1981. Externally, the TR-1A is identical to the U-2R, except for the small canted blade antenna on the upper fuselage between the engine air intakes (which has been retrofitted to many U-2Rs). (LAC)

Three of the people that made the U-2 program a success were reunited at the rollout ceremony of the first TR-1A in July of 1981; (from left) Robert Murphy, ex-State Department under President Eisenhower, Kelly Johnson, and Tony LeVier; Lockheed's Chief Test Pilot and first man to fly a U-2. (LAC)

The second TR-1A (80-1067) over southern California during an early test flight. Production TR-1As were intended to supplement the existing U-2R force and allow the Air Force to retire the remaining U-2Cs still in service. (LAC)

intelligence forces", which have been rumored to be the Nationalist Chinese, British, West Germans and Israelis, although delivery of U-2s to these nations remains unconfirmed.

With deliveries of the TR-1/U-2R assured, the Air Force began retiring its remaining U-2C aircraft. Five early U-2s were preserved and are currently on display at the Air Force Museum at Wright Patterson AFB, the March AFB Museum, SAC Museum at Offet AFB, the National Air and Space Museum in Washington, and one aircraft serves as a gate guard at Beale AFB.

TR-1 Operations

There are currently five active Air Force squadrons equipped with the U-2R/TR-1A. Four squadrons; the 4025th SRS, 4028th SRS, 99th SRS, and 4029th SRT (training) Squadron (TR-1Bs/U-2CTs) are assigned to the 9th SRW at Beale. The fifth squadron, the 95th TRS, was formed in October of 1981 under 17th TRW at RAF Alconbury, England. This squadron received its first aircraft, two TR-1As, in February of 1983, and is expected to receive a total of eighteen TR-1As for support of NATO requirements in Europe. The Beale based squadrons are responsible for all U-2 intelligence missions outside NATO and operate a mixture of TR-1As and U-2Rs.

TR-1 operations are mainly electronic intelligence missions dealing with signals intelligence (SIGINT), communications intelligence (COMINT), stand-off oblique photography, side looking radar photography, and occasionally overflights of lesser defended areas. The long endurance of the TR-1 allows the aircraft to operate for long periods outside enemy airspace gathering information on radar locations, communications centers, and other vital intelligence data.

Currently there are permanent TR-1/U-2 detachments stationed at various locations

This floodlit TR-1A reveals the graceful fuselage lines of the "jet powered glider". The wing mounted "super pods" contain a variety of sensors and TR-1/U-2Rs can carry a number of different type pods dependent on the mission. (LAC)

This TR-1A under construction shows the many different metals and composite panels used for the outer fuselage skin. Non-metallic panels and radar-absorbent paint help to reduce the radar image of the TR-1 making it harder to track by hostile radars. (LAC)

around the world, including: Korea, where Detachment (DET) 2, 9th SRW maintains one aircraft on permanent detachment at Osan Air Base; the Mediterranean area, where DET 3 maintains one TR-1A/U-2R on a rotational basis at RAF Akrotiri on Cyprus to monitor events in the Middle East and North Africa. Additionally there are currently some twenty Operating Locations (OLs) scattered around the world to which U-2Rs can be deployed in the event of increased tensions or hostile action by a potential enemy.

One such location is the island of Diego Garcia in the Indian Ocean. To support the expanded United States military presence in the Indian Ocean, TR-1/U-2Rs have been deployed to Diego Garcia as needed to monitor events in the Persian Gulf, Iran, and Afghanistan. Reportedly such quick reaction deployments are normally handled by DET 6, stationed at Norton Air Force Base, California. (Detachments 1 and 4 are based at Kadena, Okinawa and Mildenhall, England and are equipped with the SR-71 Blackbird).

TR-1A/U-2Rs of DET 5, 9th SRW, operating from Patrick AFB in Florida routinely operate off Central America. These missions are flown off the El Salvador/Nicaraguan coasts to monitor SIGINT/COMINT activity and, on occasion, TR-1/U-2Rs have made overflights of Nicaraguan facilities to photograph the extensive military build-up within this Central American nation. The photography gathered by the TR-1/U-2Rs has been used by the Reagan Administration to underscore the expansion of the Nicaraguan military with Soviet assistance. Reportedly, it was a TR-1A that revealed the presence of Soviet supplied Mi-25 Hind attack helicopters in Nicaragua.

With the advances in both fighter aircraft and surface to air missiles, TR-1 overflights are only conducted over target areas where fighter and SAM assets are lacking. Although no longer immune to interception, the TR-1 is expected to continue to serve as a valuable aerial surveillance platform well into the 1990s.

Flap Development

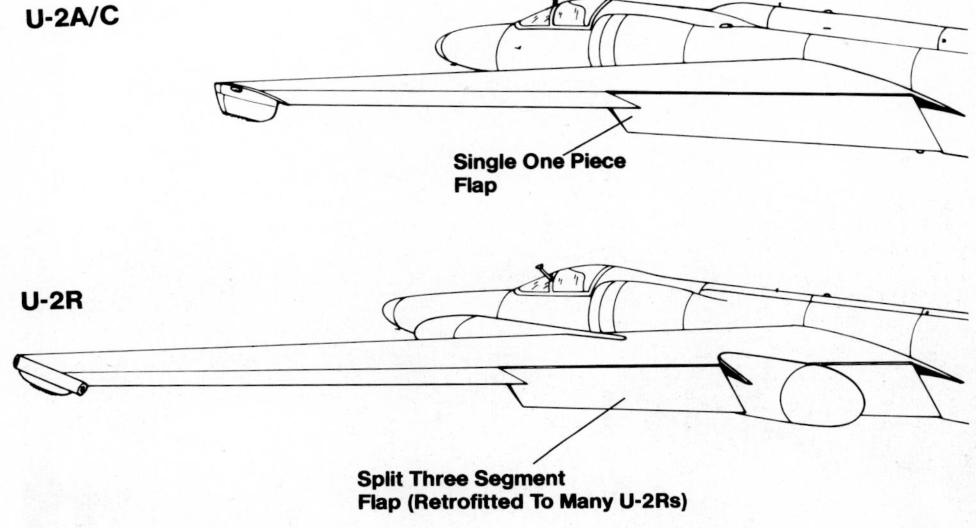

With its great expanse of wing, the TR-1A literally leaps off the runway after a short takeoff run. This same wing, however, makes landing the TR-1 difficult since the wing maintains lift at very slow airspeeds. (LAC)

A TR-1 crosses the runway threshold just prior to touchdown. The flaps on the TR-1A have three segments to allow for flexing of the long wing and split to clear the wing mounted "super pods". Early U-2Rs were equipped with single unsegmented flaps. (LAC)

(Above) This TR-1A is equipped with an ASARS radome, PLSS pods, and external rib strengtheners on the horizontal stabilizers. The TR-1A equipped with these powerful sensors remains an effective stand off surveillance aircraft and is expected to serve well into the 1990s. (LAC)

(Below) The external rib strengtheners on the horizontal stabilizers of this TR-1A were introduced when the stabilizers were discovered to be suffering from fatigue caused by aerodynamic buffeting at altitude. These external ribs are being retrofitted to both the TR-1A and U-2R during major overhauls. (LAC)

Stabilizer Ribbing

U-2R/TR-1 (Early)

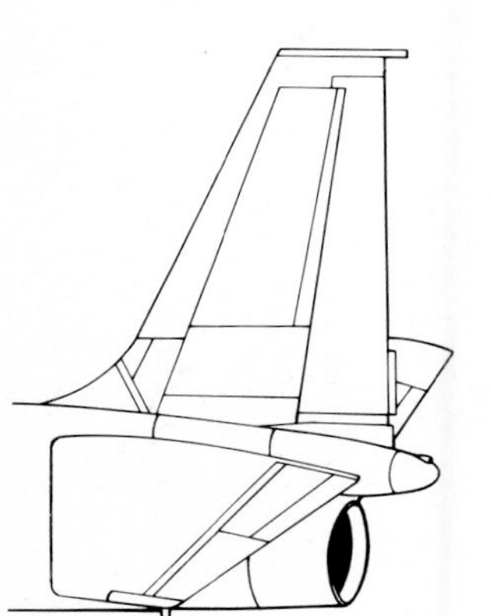

TR-1A (Late)

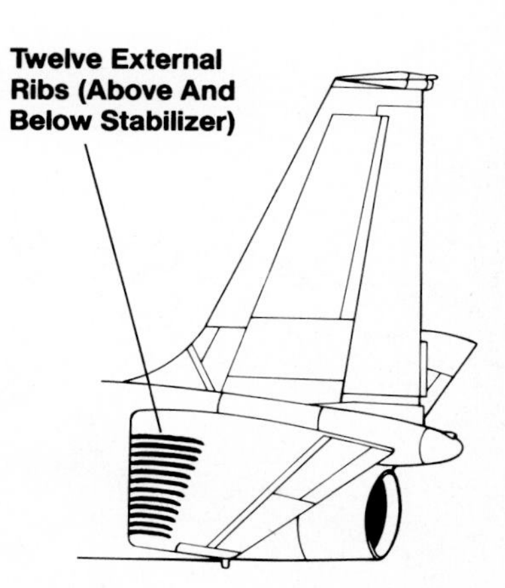

The U-2CT operates alongside the newer TR-1B in the 4029th SRTS. Both aircraft have the second cockpit mounted above and behind the standard cockpit utilizing the space normally occupied by the upper half of the equipment "Q" bay. (LAC)

The stepped rear cockpit gives the pilot an unrestricted view over the long nose of the TR-1B. Two TR-1Bs are assigned to the 4029th Strategic Reconnaissance Training Squadron at Beale AFB for crew training.

Cockpit Development

TR-1A

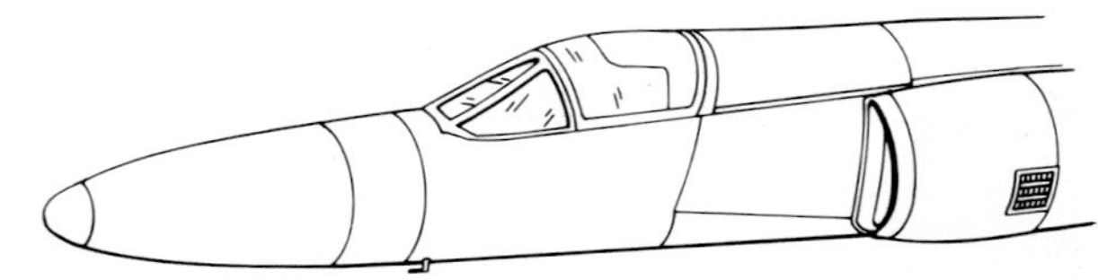

TR-1B

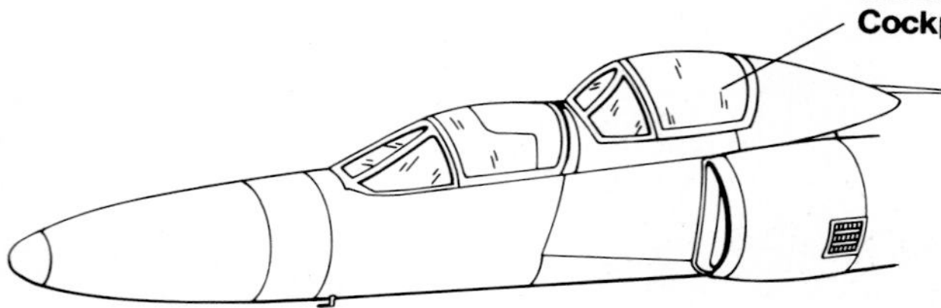

A TR-1 of the 9th SRW was deployed to Greenham Gommon Air Base, England to take part in the 25th anniversary salute to the McDonnell-Douglas F-4 Phantom during 1983. The TR-1A carries no identifying national insignia, while the SR-71A Blackbird parked next to it carries full Air Force markings. (LAC)

A TR-1B (80-1064) trainer of the 4029th SRTS at Beale AFB during early 1983. Both TR-1Bs are mission capable aircraft and could be used operationally if the need arose. (LAC)

A Mobile Control vehicle follows this TR-1 down the runway at Beale. "Mobile" advises the landing U-2 pilot of his attitude and altitude during the the final few feet of his approach since the pilot cannot visually judge his altitude above the runway. (100 SRW)

This TR-1A is equipped for optical photography with panoramic camera windows installed in the Q-Bay cover. Both outer wing panels have the Flat Black paint partially stripped for some unknown reason and the wingtips appear to have been freshly repainted. (LAC)

TR-1A/U-2R Special Mission Pods

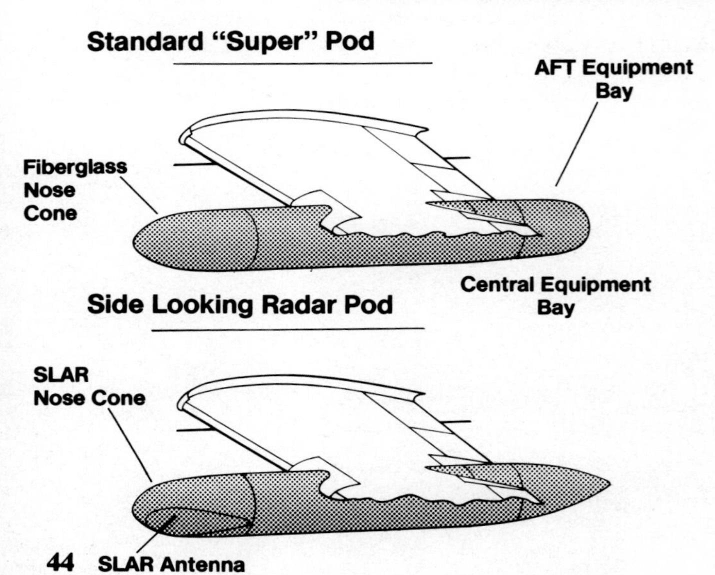

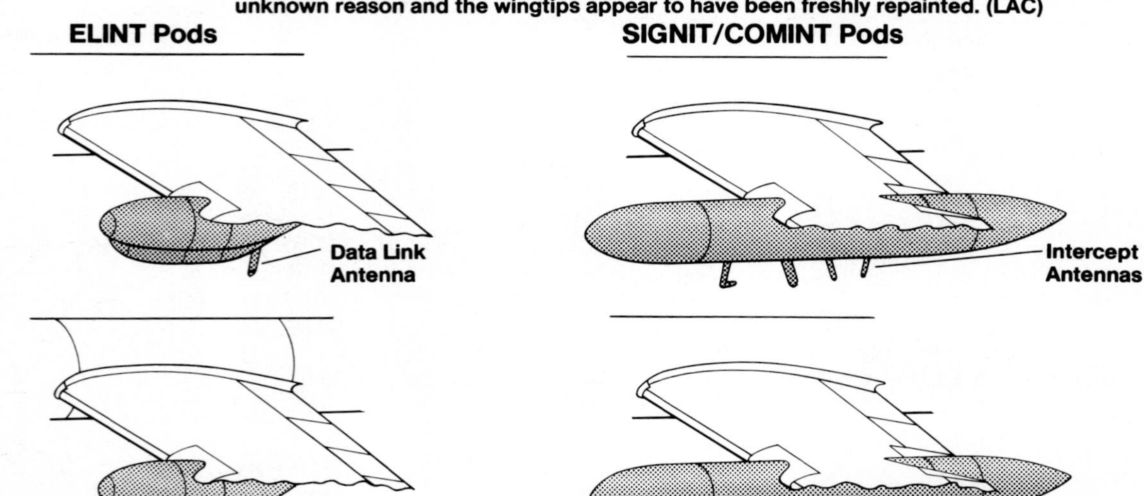

TR-1/U-2R aircraft are deployed from Beale in detachments to various locations around the world. This TR-1/U-2R of Detachment 2, 9th SRW is maneuvered out of its hangar at Osan Air Base, Korea in preparation for a mission monitoring North Korean activity along the Korean De-Militarized Zone (DMZ). (Daryl Niewald)

A TR-1A (80-1079) of the 9th SRW touches down at Beale AFB after completing another mission. The only markings normally carried by 9th SRW TR-1s is the serial number on the tail in Red.

A TR-1A/U-2R of DET 2, 9th SRW taxies in following a mission along the Korean DMZ. DET 2 maintains at least one TR-1/U-2R at Osan on a rotating basis. This aircraft is equipped with a number of ELINT antennas mounted under the rear fuselage for monitoring North Korean electronic emitters. (Tony Landis)

NASA U-2s

During the early days of the U-2 program extensive use was made of the cover story that the aircraft were National Advisory Committee for Aeronautics research aircraft. Press releases were issued by the Air Force and NACA that the Air Force Weather Service in cooperation with NACA were using the U-2 for high altitude weather research. Although some weather information was gathered by early U-2s, it was a bi-product of their intelligence mission rather than a dedicated effort. In reality, the NACA, had absolutely no control or input to the early U-2 program.

From 1955 through 1970, NACA and later its successor, the National Aeronautics and Space Administration (NASA), involvement with the U-2 was strictly a paper cover for the Central Intelligence Agency. This ended in April of 1971 when the Air Force placed on permanent loan to NASA two U-2C aircraft (N-708NA and N-709NA). Based at the Ames Research Center, Naval Air Station Moffett, California, these two U-2s were used to form the NASA High Altitude Missions Branch (HAMB). Under HAMB the aircraft were flown on a variety of earth resources projects, such as water management, land use, disaster assessment, photographic survey, and mapping.

One of the major projects undertaken by the NASA U-2Cs was the Ames Airborne Instrumentation Research Project. This project involved flights by the U-2 in conjunction with the track of the Earth Resources and Technology Satellite (ERTS). These missions collected test data for use by government, university, and industrial scientists in connection with the ERTS program. The NASA U-2s were also used to support the flight of *SKYLAB*, the manned orbiting research station.

NASA missions are unique in that all photographs and data obtained are part of the "Public Domain"; that is, open to the general public. The Ames Research Center maintains copies of all imagery, a microfilm browse file, and various light tables and viewing equipment. With prior arrangements visitors can view all NASA imagery and copy any photos they wish (with their own equipment). NASA publishes reports of each mission flown and maintains a computerized data base for all earth resources missions, this data base is also open to the public.

In June of 1982 the two NASA U-2Cs were joined by the single ER-2 (N-706NA). The ER-2 (Earth Resources-2) was the first of the TR-1 series to be produced and is basically a TR-1 with all military related systems removed. NASA's first operational mission with the ER-2 took place on 12 June 1982. Initial missions with the ER-2 were limited to pilot training and familiarization, while the aircraft's super pods were modified to accept NASA sensors. The ER-2 has an increased payload capacity of some 4,000 pounds (more than double that of the U-2C) and can carry this weight over 3,000 miles at altitudes up to 75,000 feet. The E-2R has undertaken a number of important projects at NASA, a number of which have been flown in support of the Space Shuttle program. During late 1981 the ER-2 joined the U-2Cs to complete the aerial mapping of the entire state of Alaska, producing high quality maps of previously uncharted areas.

The NASA U-2Cs have averaged approximately 100 missions per year for each aircraft and are the last early model U-2s remaining in service. It is expected that when they reach the end of their useful service lives they will be replaced by a second ER-2.

This NASA U-2C was displayed with the full complement of research equipment that can be carried on the U-2C. This U-2C (N708NA) is configured with underwing pylon mounted fuel tanks for extended range missions. (NASA via Andrews)

This U-2C (N708NA) was used to photograph large areas of the US East Coast while operating from Wallops Island, Virginia. The photographs were then compared with photos taken by the Earth Resources Technology Satellite (ERTS) as part of the satellite calibration program. (NASA via Andrews)

A NASA U-2C rests on the ramp at the Ames Research Center, Moffett Field, California during the early 1970s. NASA U-2s were painted Gloss White uppersurfaces over Light Gray (FS16473) undersurfaces with Medium Blue striping. (LAC)

The Earth Resources -2 (ER-2) during its maiden flight on 11 May 1981. The ER-2 was a demilitarized TR-1A built for NASA. The first ER-2 flew three months prior to the first TR-1A military version. (LAC)

The NASA ER-2 on final approach to the Ames Research Center at NAS Moffett Field, California. The ER-2 is not only used for atmospheric research, but has also flown fire, flood, earthquake, and volcanic damage assessment missions. (LAC)

The NASA ER-2 taxis at the Ames Research Center, Moffett, California. The aircraft is painted in the standard NASA scheme of Gloss White uppersurfaces, Gull Gray (FS 16473) fuselage underside, Medium Blue NASA striping on the fuselage sides, and Flat Black anti-glare panel on the nose. (LAC)

The mission of the ER-2 is upper atmospheric research and earth resources photography. Some of the ER-2 missions include; ozone sampling, severe storm monitoring, infrared scanning, disaster assessment, and sunspot research. The ER-2 is the sole civil research variant of the TR-1A. (LAC)